CME PROJECT

Algebra 1

Teaching Resources

PEARSON

Boston, Massachusetts
Glenview, Illinois
Shoreview, Minnesota
Upper Saddle River, New Jersey

13-digit ISBN 978-0-13-364426-5

10-digit ISBN 0-13-364426-X

3 4 5 6 7 8 9 10   11 10 09

Contents

Instructional Support Blackline Masters

Chapter 4 Instructional Support

Chapter 5 Instructional Support

Chapter 6 Instructional Support

Chapter 7 Instructional Support

Chapter 8 Instructional Support

Additional Practice Blackline Masters

Chapter 1 Additional Practice

Chapter 2 Additional Practice

Chapter 3 Additional Practice

Chapter 4 Additional Practice

Chapter 5 Additional Practice

Chapter 6 Additional Practice

Chapter 7 Additional Practice

Chapter 8 Additional Practice

Answers to Practice Workbook

Number Lines

←————————————————————————————————→

←————————————————————————————————→

←————————————————————————————————→

←————————————————————————————————→

←————————————————————————————————→

←————————————————————————————————→

←————————————————————————————————→

Alternate Number Lines

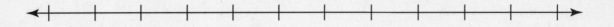

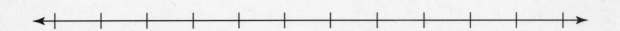

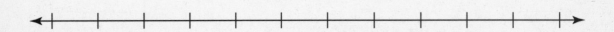

Name _____ Class _____ Date _____

Graph Paper

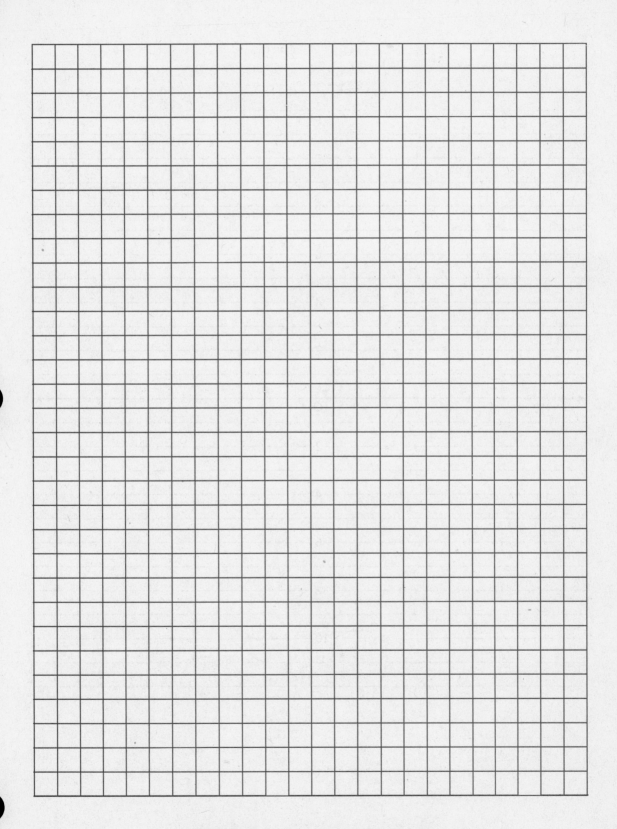

Coordinate Plane

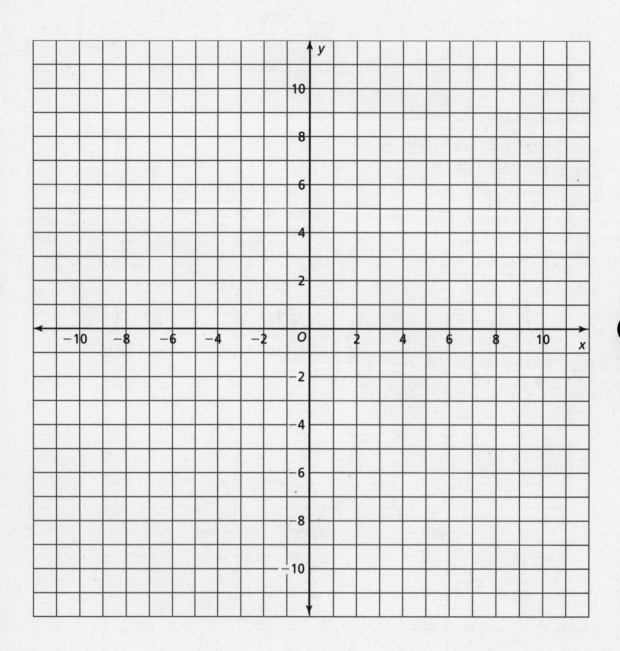

Two-Column Table

Addition Table

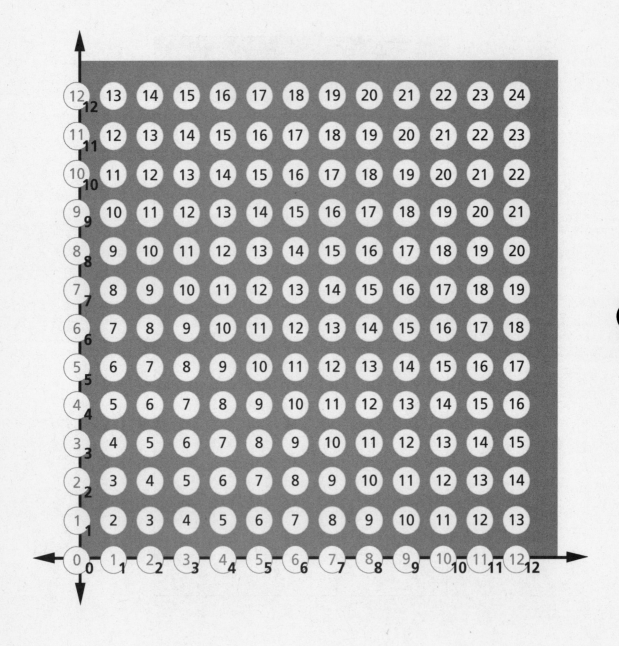

Multiplication Table

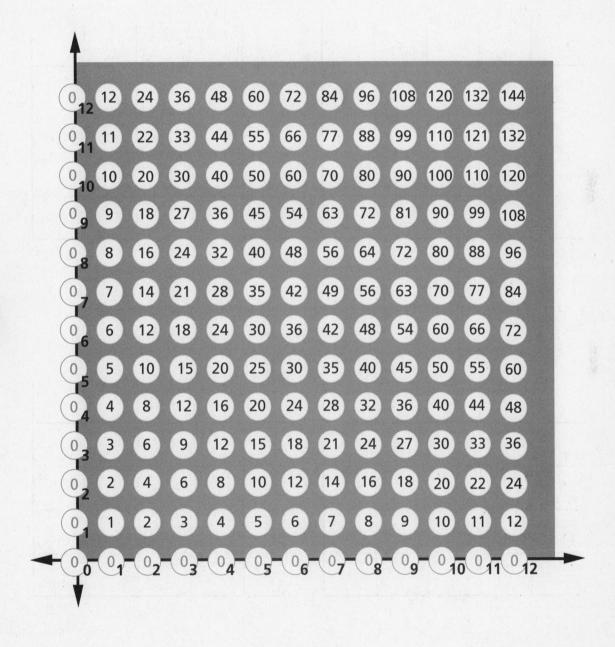

Expansion Boxes

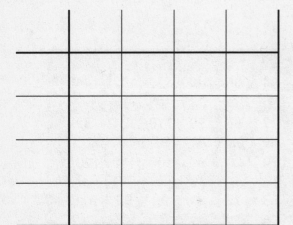

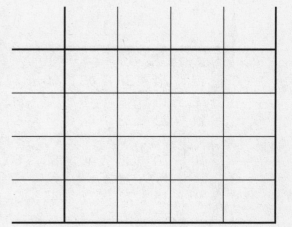

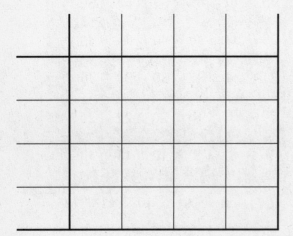

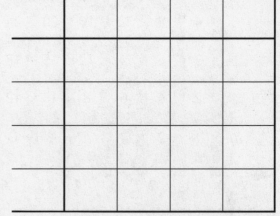

Input-Output Tables

Input	Output

Input	Output

Input	Output

Input	Output

Input	Output

Input	Output

Input	Output

Input	Output

Input	Output

Function Machines

input *x*

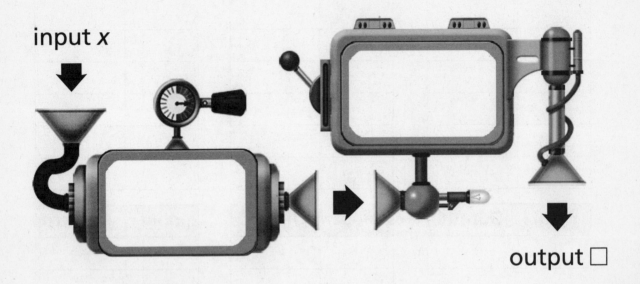

output □

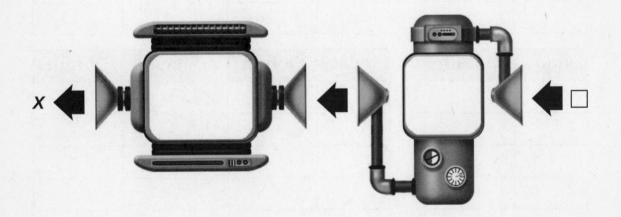

x

□

Difference Tables

Input	Output	Δ

Input	Output	Δ

Input	Output	Δ

Input	Output	Δ

Input	Output	Δ

Input	Output	Δ

Input	Output	Δ

Input	Output	Δ

Input	Output	Δ

Error Table

Input	Actual	Predicted	Error

Distance-Time Graph

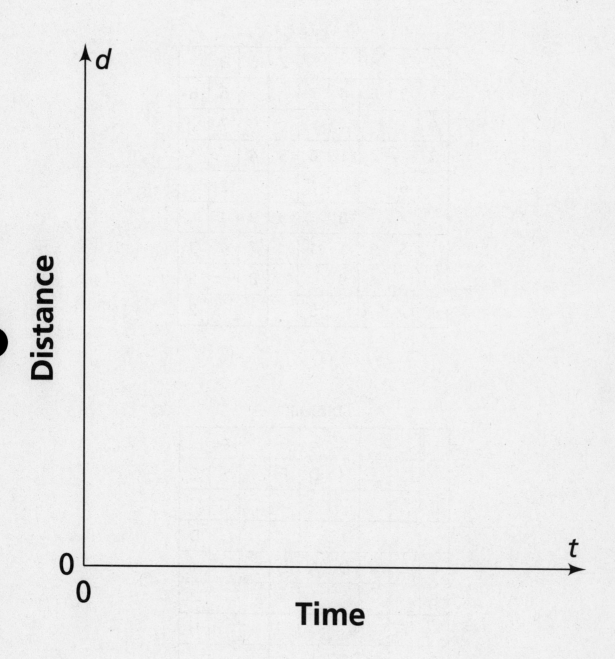

Habits of Mind Experiments 1

Sudoku Tables

Easy

4	7	8			2	6	3	
2	3	6	4	7			5	8
9	1						7	
3		2	1	6	5	4		
	6						2	
			8		9	3	1	
	5	9		1		7		3
		4	9			8		5
				5		1		2

Difficult

			B		G		A	
			H	D	F			C
D						G		
								D
C			D	A	E			I
B								
	F							H
A			G	I	C			
	E		A		H			

Habits of Mind Experiments 2

Cross-sums Tables

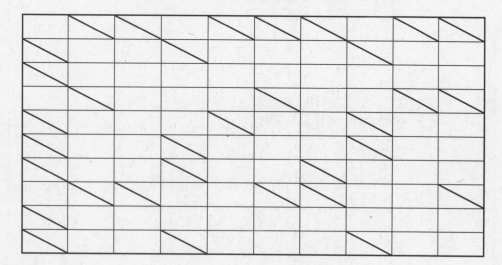

Dodgeball Tables

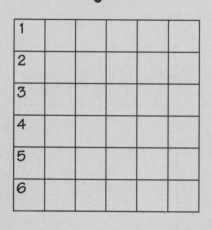

Player A

1					
2					
3					
4					
5					
6					

Player B

1	2	3	4	5	6

Addition–Multiplication Table

Blackline Master 1.1

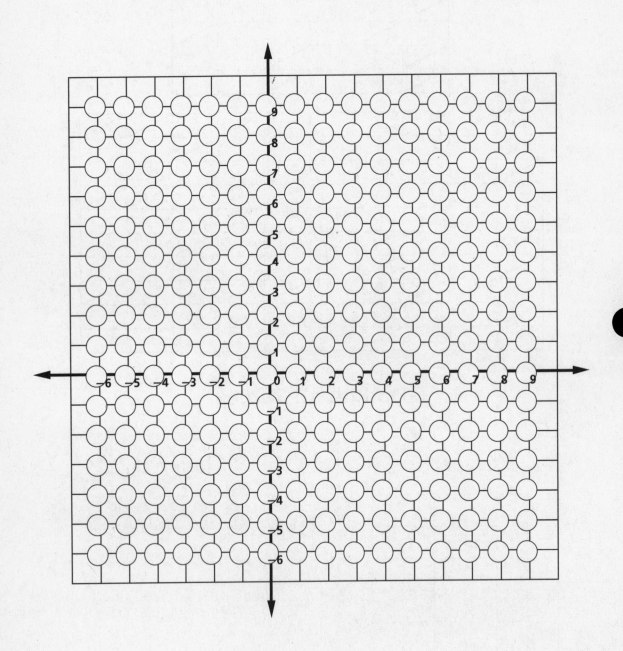

Checkbook

Number	Date	Purpose	Payment Amount	✓	Deposit Amount	Balance

Extended Addition Table

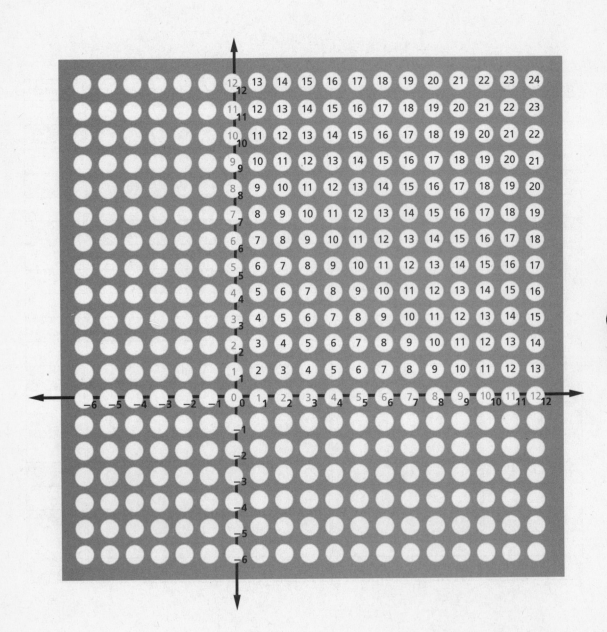

Extended Multiplication Table

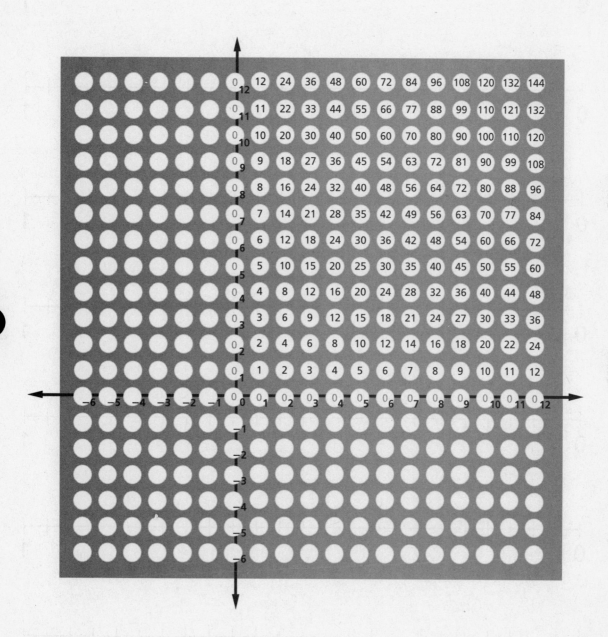

Seven Line Segments

0   1

0   1

0   1

0   1

0   1

0   1

0   1

Ruler

Visualizing Fractions

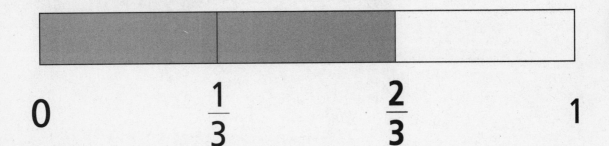

one sixth

one half

0        $\dfrac{1}{3}$ $\dfrac{2}{3}$ 1

0    $\dfrac{1}{6}$ $\dfrac{2}{6}$ $\dfrac{3}{6}$ $\dfrac{4}{6}$ $\dfrac{5}{6}$ 1

Multiplying Two Numbers

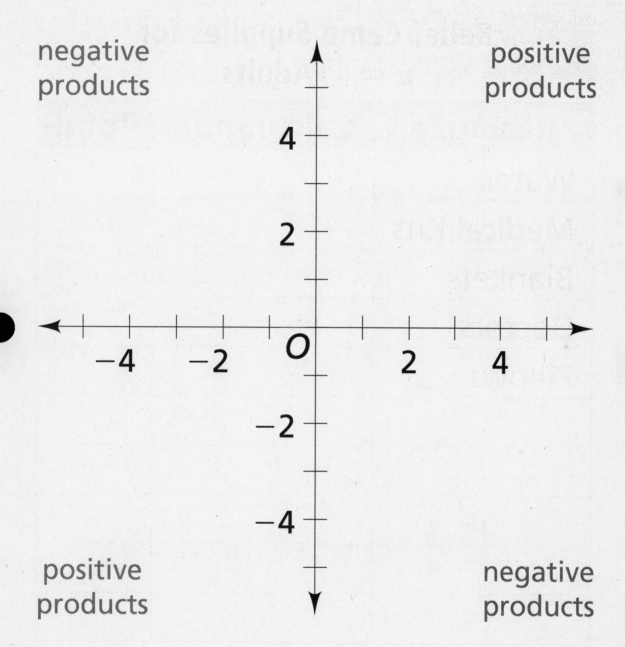

negative
products

positive
products

positive
products

negative
products

Relief Camp Supplies Table

Relief Camp Supplies for
$a = \square$ Adults

Resource	Calculation	Total
Water		
Medical Kits		
Blankets		
Doctors		
Pillows		

Input-Output Table

Input, x	Output, x^2
-4	16
-3	
-2	
-1	
0	
1	
2	
3	9
4	

Solving $3t + 12 = 5t + 6$

$$3t + 12 = 5t + 6$$

$$12 = 2t + 6$$

Solving for x

Rebecca

$40 - 4(x + 3) = 7x - 5$

$40 - 4x + 12 = 7x - 5$

$52 - 4x = 7x - 5$

$57 - 4x + 5 = 7x - 5 + 5$

$57 - 4x = 7x$

$57 - 4x + 4x = 7x + 4x$

$57 = 11x$

$\dfrac{57}{11} = x$

Anna

$40 - 4(x + 3) = 7x - 5$

$40 - 4x + 3 = 7x - 5$

$43 - 4x = 7x - 5$

$39x = 7x - 5$

$39x - 7x = 7x - 5 - 7x$

$32x = -5$

$x = -\dfrac{5}{32}$

Jenna

$40 - 4(x + 3) = 7x - 5$

$40 - 4x - 12 = 7x - 5$

$28 - 4x = 7x - 5$

$28 - 4x + 4x = 7x - 5 + 4x$

$28 = 11x - 5$

$28 + 5 = 11x - 5 + 5$

$33 = 11x$

$3 = x$

Who has the correct result?
What mistakes did each of the others make?

Guess-Check-Generalize Notebook   Blackline Master 2.15

Check	Step
1	
2	
3	
4	
5	

Point-Coordinates Table and Graph **Blackline Master 3.1**

Point	Coordinates
E	
O	
	(0, 1)
C	(3, 2)
J	
	(2.5, −2.5)
M	
	(−2.5,)
D	
B	
G	$\left(-\frac{1}{2}, -3\right)$
	(1, 0)
A	
F	

Best Actor and Actress Table

Winners Best Actor and Best Actress Awards

Year	Age	Best Actor	Best Actress	Age
1986	61	Paul Newman	Marlee Matlin	21
1987	43	Michael Douglas	Cher	41
1988	51	Dustin Hoffman	Jodie Foster	26
1989	32	Daniel Day-Lewis	Jessica Tandy	80
1990	42	Jeremy Irons	Kathy Bates	42
1991	54	Anthony Hopkins	Jodie Foster	29
1992	52	Al Pacino	Emma Thompson	33
1993	37	Tom Hanks	Holly Hunter	35
1994	38	Tom Hanks	Jessica Lange	45
1995	31	Nicolas Cage	Susan Sarandon	49
1996	45	Geoffrey Rush	Frances McDormand	39
1997	60	Jack Nicholson	Helen Hunt	34
1998	46	Roberto Benigni	Gwyneth Paltrow	26
1999	40	Kevin Spacey	Hilary Swank	25
2000	36	Russell Crowe	Julia Roberts	33
2001	47	Denzel Washington	Halle Berry	35
2002	29	Adrien Brody	Nicole Kidman	35
2003	43	Sean Penn	Charlize Theron	28
2004	37	Jamie Foxx	Hilary Swank	30
2005	38	Philip Seymour Hoffman	Reese Witherspoon	29
2006	45	Forest Whitaker	Helen Mirren	61

SOURCE: Academy of Motion Pictures Arts and Sciences

Histogram

0

Best Actor Winner Displays

Histogram

Winners of Best Actor in a Leading Role

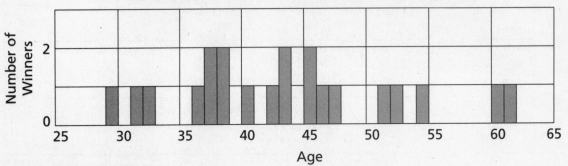

SOURCE: Academy of Motion Pictures Arts and Sciences

Stem-and-Leaf Display

Ages of Winners of Best
Actor in a Leading Role

```
2 | 9
3 | 1 2 6 7 7 8 8
4 | 0 2 3 3 5 5 6 7
5 | 1 2 4
6 | 0 1
```

Key: 2 | 9 means 29 years

Elapsed Time Estimates Table

Time 1	Time 2	Time 1	Time 2
28	36	29	31
26	35	24	27
7	27	23	32
24	28	29	26
26	37	31	34
14	30	24	31

Elapsed Time Estimate Plot

Box-and-Whisker Plot

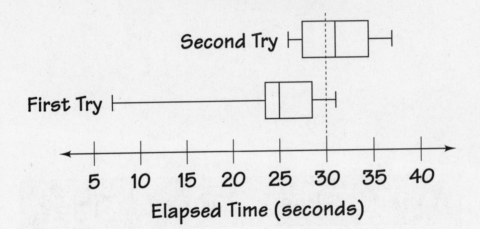

Box-and-Whisker Plot

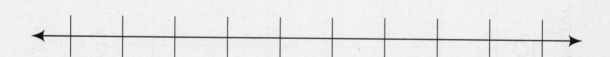

Scatter Plot

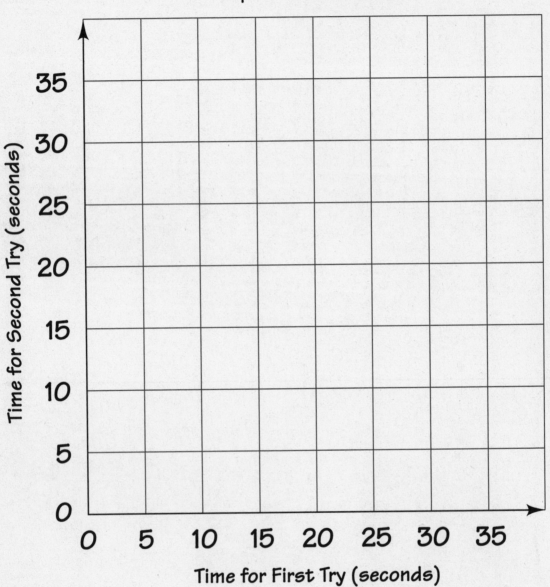

Elapsed Time Estimates

Time for Second Try (seconds)

Time for First Try (seconds)

(*x*, *y*) Tables with Coordinate Planes Blackline Master 3.10

x	y	(x, y)
1	4	(1, 4)
2		
−3		
	0	
$\frac{1}{2}$		
	−2	
	$-\frac{11}{3}$	

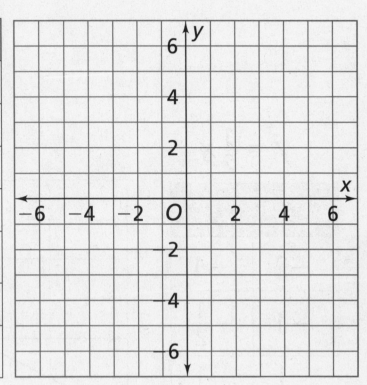

x	y	(x, y)

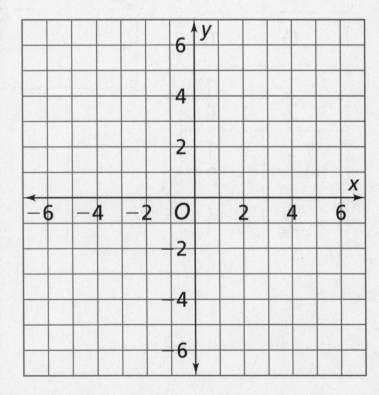

Direct Variation, y = cx

$$y = \frac{1}{2}x$$

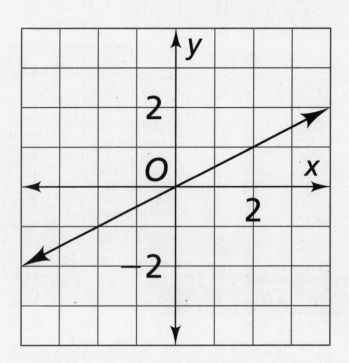

x	y
−2	−1
−1	$-\frac{1}{2}$
$-\frac{1}{2}$	$-\frac{1}{4}$
0	0
$\frac{1}{2}$	$\frac{1}{4}$
1	$\frac{1}{2}$
2	1

Inverse Variation, $xy = c$

$$y = \frac{6}{x}$$

x	y
−6	−1
−3	−2
−1	−6
−$\frac{1}{2}$	−12
0	undefined
−$\frac{1}{2}$	12
1	6
3	2
6	1

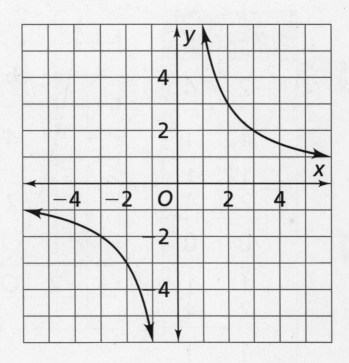

Quadratic, $y = x^2$

$y = x^2$

x	y
−2	4
−1	1
$-\frac{1}{2}$	$\frac{1}{4}$
0	0
$\frac{1}{2}$	$\frac{1}{4}$
1	1
2	4

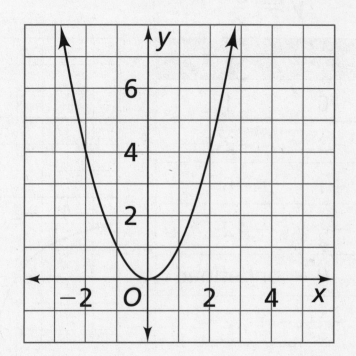

Cubic, $y = x^3$

$$y = x^3$$

x	y
−2	−8
−1	−1
$-\frac{1}{2}$	$-\frac{1}{8}$
0	0
$\frac{1}{2}$	$\frac{1}{8}$
1	1
2	8

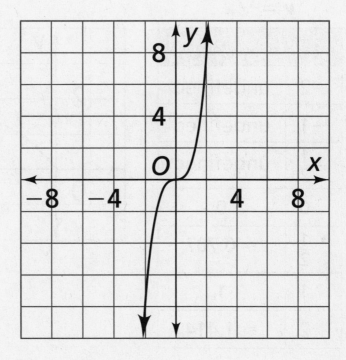

Square Root, $y = \sqrt{x}$

$$y = \sqrt{x}$$

x	y
−2	undefined
−1	undefined
$-\frac{1}{2}$	undefined
0	0
$\frac{1}{2}$	≈ 0.707
1	1
2	≈ 1.414

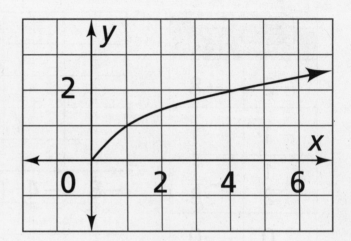

Absolute Value, $y = |x|$

$y = |x|$

x	y
−2	2
−1	1
$-\frac{1}{2}$	$\frac{1}{2}$
0	0
$\frac{1}{2}$	$\frac{1}{2}$
1	1
2	2

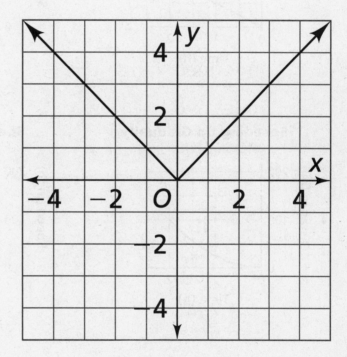

Distance and Speed Relationships   Blackline Master 4.3A

Moving Steadily

Distance (mi) vs Time (h)

Moving Steadily

Speed (mph) vs Time (h)

Speeding Up Gradually

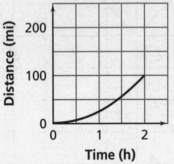

Speeding Up Gradually

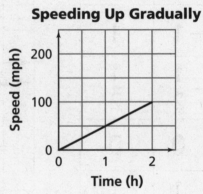

Slowing Down Gradually

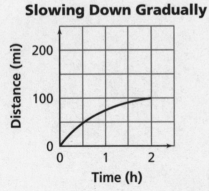

Slowing Down Gradually

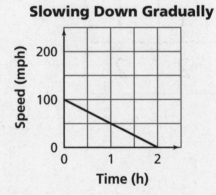

Graphs of Ball's Path and Speed

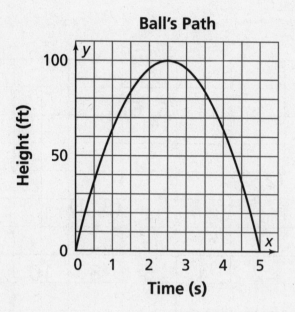

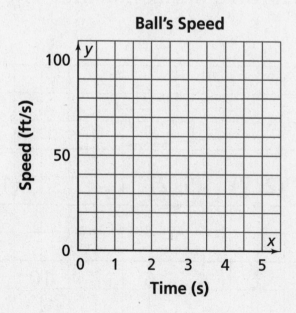

Collinear Points

These points appear to form a triangle. They are not collinear.

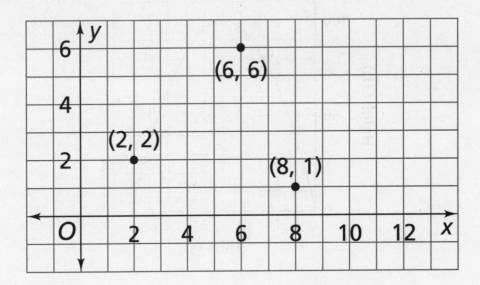

These points lie on a horizontal line. They are collinear.

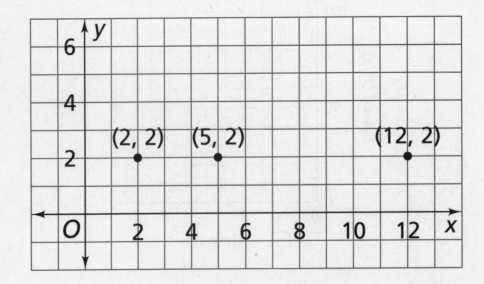

Collinearity on a Graph

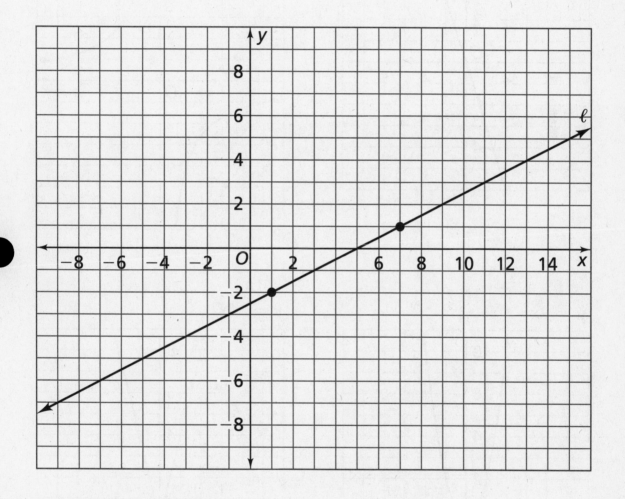

Comparing Slopes

$y = 3x$

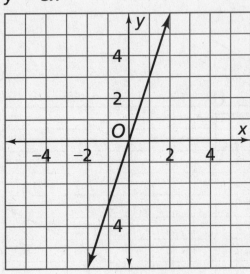

$y = \dfrac{5}{x}$

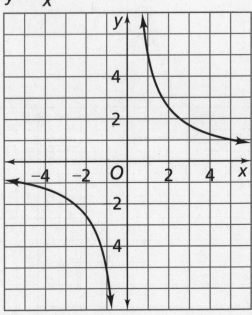

$y = 2x^2$

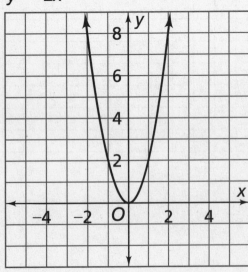

$y = |4x|$

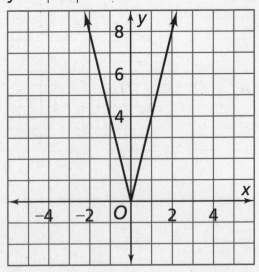

Intersection of Lines

Blackline Master 4.10

a.

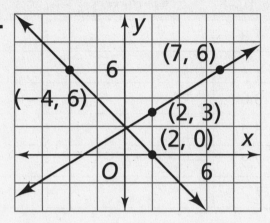

b.

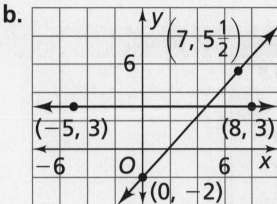

c.

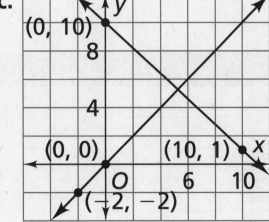

Error Tables

Input	Actual	Predicted	Error
1	1.8		
2	1.7		
3	3.6		
5	5.4		
6	7.3		
7	7.2		

Input	Actual	Predicted	Error
1	1.8		
2	1.7		
3	3.6		
5	5.4		
6	7.3		
7	7.2		

Input	Actual	Predicted	Error
1	1.8		
2	1.7		
3	3.6		
5	5.4		
6	7.3		
7	7.2		

Items to Purchase Now

Item	Price Original	Price Discounted	Tax (5%)	Shipping Cost	Total Cost
Ultimate Broadway	$12.98			$2.00	
Greatest Movie Songs	$14.99			$2.00	
Patriotic Medley	$11.98			$2.00	
Top Country Hits	$16.98			$2.00	
A History of Soul	$18.98			$2.00	
90s Favorites	$ 5.89			$2.00	

Charity Run Donations

Number of Miles	Mom	Uncle	Teacher	Coach	Agustina	Total Donation
1			$10.00		$5.00	
2			$10.00		$5.00	
3			$10.00		$5.00	
4			$10.00		$5.00	
5			$10.00		$5.00	

Function Tables 1

Input	Output
0	
1	
−2	
5	
	7

Input	Output
0	
1	
−2	
5	
	7

$f(x) = -2x + 5$ **Blackline Master 5.4**

Input, x	Output, $f(x)$
0	
1	3
2	
3	
4	−3
5	

Rule C and Rule D

Rule C

Input, n	Output
0	5
1	10
2	
3	
4	
5	

Rule D

Input, x	Output
0	5
1	10
2	
3	
4	
5	

Roof Plan

Roof Plan

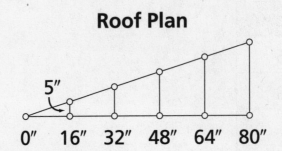

Distance From End (in.)	Length of Board (in.)
16	5
32	
48	
64	
80	

Linear Function with Variable *a*

Input	Output	Δ
0	3	a
1		a
2		a
3		a
4	$4a + 3$	a
5		

Linear Function with *a* and *b*

Input	Output	Δ
0	*b*	*a*
1		*a*
2		*a*
3		*a*
4	4*a* + *b*	*a*
5		

Function Tables 2

a.

Input	Output	Δ
0		6
1		6
2		6
3		6
4	13	6
5		

b.

Input	Output	Δ
0	1	
1	3	
2	9	
3	27	
4	81	
5	243	

c.

Input	Output	Δ
0	-2	
1	$-\frac{6}{5}$	
2	$-\frac{2}{5}$	
3	$\frac{2}{5}$	$\frac{4}{5}$
4	$\frac{6}{5}$	
5	2	

d.

Input	Output	Δ
0		-2
1		-2
2	5	-2
3		-2
4		-2
5		

Linear Function Tables

a.

Input	Output	Δ
0	5	
1	8	
2	11	
3	14	
4	17	

b.

Input	Output	Δ
0	−7	
1	−4	
2	−1	
3	2	
4	5	

c.

Input	Output	Δ
0	12	
1	9	
2	6	
3	3	
4	0	

d.

Input	Output	Δ
0	*r*	*s*
1		*s*
2		*s*
3		*s*
4		

Bank E

Bank E

Year	James's Savings	Interest
0	$85	$4.25
1		
2		
3		
4		
5		

Matchsticks Table

Matchsticks Table

Stage	Number of Matchsticks
1	4
2	7
3	
4	
5	

Function Tables 3

a.

Input	Output	Δ
0		3
1		3
2		3
3		3
4	14	3
5		

b.

Input	Output	Δ
0	5	
1	2	
2	−1	
3	−4	
4	−7	
5	−10	

Adam's Earnings

Weeks, w	Adam's Earnings, $T(w)$
1	
2	
3	
4	
5	
6	

Payment Options

Payment Options: $1000 Balance at 12% Interest

Payment	Months to Pay	Total Payments	Interest
$10			
$15			
$20			
$25			
$30			
$40			
$50	22	$1121.36	$121.36
$60			
$75			
$100			

Kara's Account Balance

Kara's Account Balance

Month	Starting Balance	Interest	Deposit	Ending Balance
0	$0	$0	$ 0	$0
1	$0		$50	
2			$50	
3			$50	

Ratio Tables

x	3^x	$\div$
-3		
-2		
-1		
0		
1		
2		
3		

x	$\left(\dfrac{1}{3}\right)^x$	$\div$
-3		
-2		
-1		
0		
1		
2		
3		

Multiplication Table

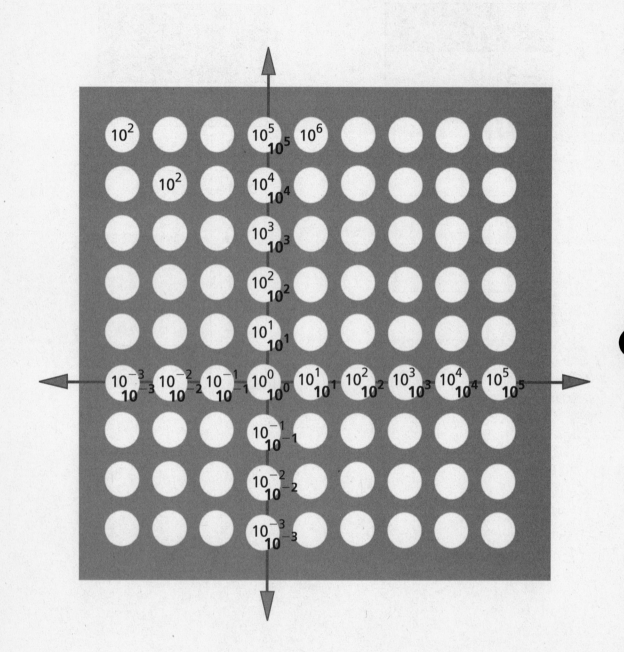

Venn Diagram of Number Sets

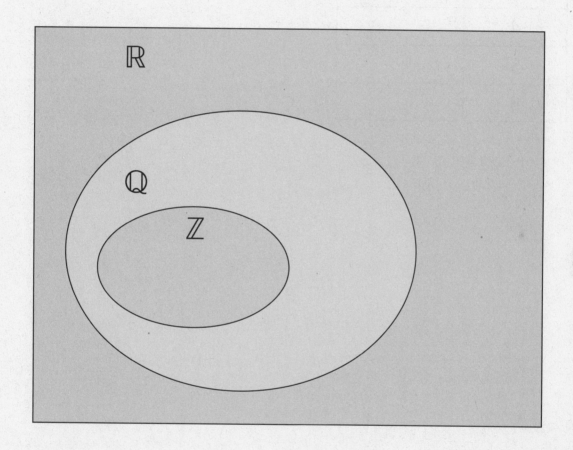

Guess-a-Number Table

Guess, g	Number, N
1	1
2	3
3	7
4	
5	
6	

Input-Output Tables

a. $f(a) = 3 \cdot 2^a$

Input, a	Output, $f(a)$
0	
1	
2	
3	
4	

b. $g(a) = 2 \cdot 5^a$

Input, a	Output, $g(a)$
0	
1	
2	
3	
4	

c. $h(a) = 27 \cdot 3^{-a}$

Input, a	Output, $h(a)$
0	
1	
2	
3	
4	

d. $j(a) = 27 \cdot \left(\frac{1}{3}\right)^a$

Input, a	Output, $j(a)$
0	
1	
2	
3	
4	

Guess-for-*N* Table

Guess, *N* (years)	Account Balance ($)	The actual *N* is . . .	The next guess should be . . .

Doubling Time Table

APR (%)	Number of Years Needed to Double Investment
3	
4	
5	
6	12
7	
8	
9	
10	
12	

Toss and Survivor Table

Toss Number	Number of Survivors
0	40
1	
2	
3	
4	
5	
6	

Toss Number	Number of Survivors
0	40
1	
2	
3	
4	
5	
6	

Bouncing Ball Table

Bounce Height

Bounce, b	Height, h (ft)
0	18
1	12
2	8
3	
4	
5	

Finding a Function Rule

Stage 1

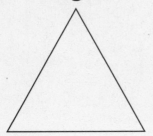

Stage 2

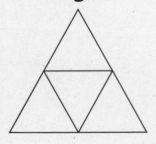

Stage 3

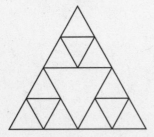

Stage	Number of Upward-Pointing Triangles
1	1
2	3
3	
4	

Area of a Figure 1

Area of a Figure 2

Area of a Figure 3

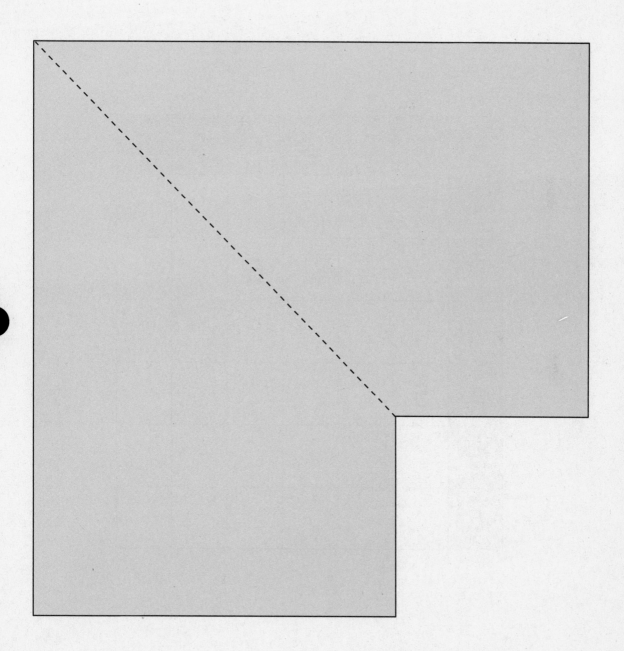

Sums of Two Number Cubes 1 **Blackline Master 7.5A**

	1	2	3	4	5	6
1						
2				6		
3						
4	5					
5						
6						

Sums of Two Number Cubes 2 _____ **Blackline Master 7.5B**

	1	3	4	5	6	8
1						
2				7		
2						
3		6				
3						
4						

Sum and Product Table 1

Numbers With a Given Sum and Product		
Sum of Two Numbers	**Product of Two Numbers**	**Numbers**
20	99	11 and 9
20	96	
20	75	
20	36	
20	-125	
20	47	
20	n	

Name _____ Class _____ Date _____

Sum and Product Table 2

Numbers With a Given Sum and Product		
Sum of Two Numbers	**Product of Two Numbers**	**Numbers**
100	2500	50 and 50
100	2491	53 and 47
100	2484	
100	2451	
100	2379	
100	2211	
100	−309	
100	1234	
100	n	

7 × 7 Square

Difference of Squares Table

	0^2	1^2	2^2	3^2	4^2	5^2	6^2	7^2	8^2	9^2	10^2
10^2	100		96								
9^2	81								17		
8^2	64										
7^2	49			33							
6^2	36										
5^2	25										
4^2	16										
3^2	9										
2^2	4	3	0								
1^2	1	0									
0^2	0										

Number of Ways Table

Integer	Number of Ways	Difference
1	1	1 − 0
2	0	none

Name _____ Class _____ Date _____

Solving Quadratics

$2x^2 + 7x + 4 = 0$

$2x^2 - 7x + 4 = 0$

$$x^2 - \frac{7}{2}x + 2 = 0$$

$$x^2 - \frac{7}{2}x + \left(\frac{49}{16} - \frac{49}{16}\right) + 2 = 0$$

$$\left(x^2 - \frac{7}{2}x + \frac{49}{16}\right) - \frac{49}{16} + 2 = 0$$

$$\left(x - \frac{7}{4}\right)^2 - \frac{17}{16} = 0$$

$$\left(\left(x - \frac{7}{4}\right) - \sqrt{\frac{17}{16}}\right)\left(\left(x - \frac{7}{4}\right) + \sqrt{\frac{17}{16}}\right) = 0$$

$$x - \frac{7}{4} - \frac{\sqrt{17}}{4} = 0 \text{ or } x - \frac{7}{4} + \frac{\sqrt{17}}{4} = 0$$

$$x = \frac{7}{4} + \frac{\sqrt{17}}{4} \text{ or } x = \frac{7}{4} - \frac{\sqrt{17}}{4}$$

$$x = \frac{7 \pm \sqrt{17}}{4}$$

Rectangular Pens

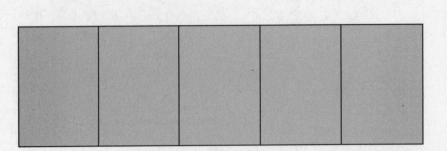

Parabolas

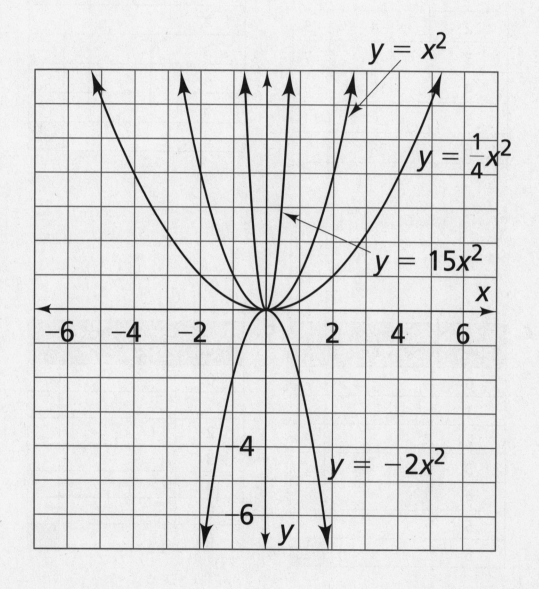

$y = x^2$

$y = \frac{1}{4}x^2$

$y = 15x^2$

$y = -2x^2$

Difference Tables

a.

Input, x	Output, x^2	Δ
0	0	
1	1	
2	4	5
3	9	7
4	16	
5		11
6	36	

b.

Input, x	Output, $2x^2$	Δ
0		
1		
2		
3		
4		
5		
6		

c.

Input, x	Output, $3x^2 - 6x - 1$	Δ
0		
1		
2		
3		
4		
5		
6		

d.

Input, x	Output, $9 - x^2$	Δ
0		
1		
2		
3		
4		
5		
6		

Difference Table

Input	Output	Δ
0		−3
1		−1
2		1
3		3
4		5
5		7
6		

Graph of $y = x^3 - x$

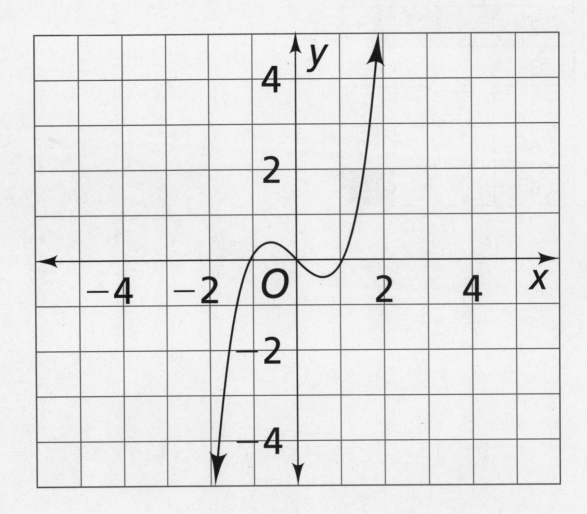

Extended Difference Table

Input	Output	Δ	
0	0		
1	3		
2	8		
3	15		
4	24		
5	35		
6	48		

Fitting a Quadratic to a Table

Input	Output			
0	1			
1	10			
2	29			
3	58			
4	97			

$v(x) = (x - 1)(x - 3)(x - 6)$

x	v(x)	Δ	Δ²
0	−18		
1	0		
2	4		
3	0		
4	−6		
5	−8		
6	0		
7	24		

Difference Table for $D(n)$

n	$D(n)$	Δ
0	1	
1	2	
2	4	
3	8	
4	16	
5	32	
6	64	

Additional Practice

For Exercises 1–4, start with each number given. Then add 5, subtract 11, subtract 8, and add 3. Fill in the ending number.

	Starting Number	Ending Number
1.	20	☐
2.	2	☐
3.	0	☐
4.	−5	☐

5. Write a simpler recipe explaining how to go from the starting number to the ending number for Exercises 1–4.

For Exercises 6–13, find each difference. Do not use a calculator.

6. $87 - 49$ **7.** $87 - 59$ **8.** $87 - 69$ **9.** $87 - 79$

10. $87 - 89$ **11.** $87 - 99$ **12.** $87 - 109$ **13.** $87 - 119$

14. Identify a pattern in the last digit of the results for Exercises 6–13.

For Exercises 15–18, state whether each equation is *true* or *false*.

15. $108 - (-153) \stackrel{?}{=} 108 + 153$ **16.** $217 - (123 + 17) \stackrel{?}{=} 217 - 123 + 17$

17. $75 + (-218) \stackrel{?}{=} 75 - 218$ **18.** $393 - (251 + 83) \stackrel{?}{=} 393 - 251 - 83$

For Exercises 19–22, calculate each sum. Do not use a calculator.

19. $2 + (-9)$ **20.** $11 + (-13)$ **21.** $7 + (-10)$ **22.** $(-7) + (-12)$

For Exercises 23–24, determine whether each statement is *true* or *false*. Explain using examples to support your claim.

23. The sum of a positive integer and a positive integer is positive.

24. The sum of a positive integer and a negative integer is negative.

For Exercises 25–28, find the opposite of each number.

25. 7   **26.** −23   **27.** −1   **28.** 0

Additional Practice

For Exercises 1–8, find each result.

1. $91 \cdot 13$

2. $(-91) \cdot 13$

3. $(-91) \div 13$

4. $(-91) \div (-13)$

5. $(-91) \cdot (-13)$

6. $91 \div 13$

7. $91 \div (-13)$

8. $91 \cdot (-13)$

9. What pair of numbers with a sum of 15 has the greatest product? What pair has the least positive product?

For Exercises 10–11, determine whether each statement is *true* or *false*. Explain using examples to support your claim.

10. The product of two numbers with the same sign is always negative.

11. The product of two numbers with different signs is always negative.

For Exercises 12–15, use the basic rules of arithmetic to rewrite each calculation more simply. Then find each product.

12. $(5 \cdot 82) \cdot 2$

13. $29 \cdot 36$

14. $18 \cdot 701$

15. $22 \cdot 53$

For Exercises 16–24, find each result. Do not use a calculator.

16. $14 \cdot (-5) + (-3)$

17. $14 \cdot (5) - (-3)$

18. $14 + (-5 \cdot 3)$

19. $14 - (-5 \cdot (-3))$

20. $14 + (-5 - (-3))$

21. $14 - (5 \cdot (-3))$

22. $3(6 - 1) + 3(6 - 2) + 3(6 - 3) + 3(6 - 4)$

23. $3(5 - 1) + 3(5 - 2) + 3(5 - 3) + 3(5 - 4)$

24. $3(4 - 1) + 3(4 - 2) + 3(4 - 3) + 3(4 - 4)$

Additional Practice

1. Three bowling balls have finger holes with diameters $\frac{13}{32}$ inch, $\frac{19}{32}$ inch, and $\frac{25}{32}$ inch. A finger hole with diameter $\frac{3}{4}$ inch is slightly too large for you. Which bowling ball should you try next? Explain.

For Exercises 2–5, match each number to a point on the number line.

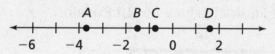

2. $-\frac{3}{2}$ 3. $-\frac{15}{4}$ 4. $\frac{5}{3}$ 5. $\frac{-5}{6}$

For Exercises 6–11, identify the fractions equivalent to -6.

6. $\frac{-3}{18}$ 7. $\frac{-42}{-7}$ 8. $\frac{-42}{7}$

9. $\frac{60}{-10}$ 10. $\frac{-6}{6}$ 11. $\frac{24}{4}$

For Exercises 12–15, convert each decimal to a fraction in lowest terms.

12. 0.15   13. -2.79 14. 4.50   15. 0.61

16. Fill in the missing labels on the number line.

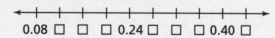

17. **Multiple Choice** Choose the pair of numbers that makes the inequality $\square < \sqrt{27} \leq \square$ true.
  A. 4.5 and 5.0   **B.** 5.0 and 5.5   **C.** 5.5 and 6.0   **D.** 6.0 and 6.5

For Exercises 18–23, state whether each number is between 3 and 4 on the number line.

18. $\frac{13}{4}$ 19. $\frac{23}{8}$ 20. $\frac{11}{3}$

21. $\frac{391}{100}$ 22. $\frac{40}{9}$ 23. $\frac{-4}{20}$

Name _____ Class _____ Date _____

Additional Practice

For Exercises 1–6, illustrate each sum on a number line.

1. $-5 + 8$ **2.** $1\frac{3}{4} + \frac{3}{4}$ **3.** $-3 + 0$

4. $(-2) + (-4)$ **5.** $5 + (-3)$ **6.** $(-3) + \left(-\frac{2}{3}\right)$

7. What is wrong with this illustration for $6 + (-4)$? Explain.

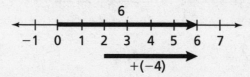

For Exercises 8–11, locate each point on the number line.

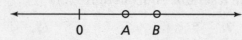

8. $B + A$ **9.** $A + A$ **10.** $A - B$ **11.** $-A$

For Exercises 12–14, find each product using the distributive property.

12. $20 \cdot \left(\frac{3}{10} + \frac{3}{4}\right)$ **13.** $8 \cdot \left(\frac{5}{8} + \frac{1}{2}\right)$ **14.** $6 \cdot \left(\frac{2}{3} + \frac{1}{2}\right)$

For Exercises 15–17, fill in each blank with a number that makes the equation true.

15. $5 \cdot \left(\frac{1}{2} + \square\right) = 4$

16. $-\frac{1}{4} \cdot (6 + \square) = -\frac{15}{4}$

17. $-7 \cdot \left(\frac{5}{9} + \square\right) = 0$

For Exercises 18–21, *A* and *B* are the two points on the number line represented by the open circles. Match each of the black points with one of the following labels.

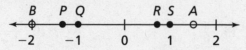

18. $\frac{A}{2}$ **19.** $\frac{1}{A} \cdot A$ **20.** $\frac{2}{3} \cdot B$ **21.** $B + 1$

Additional Practice

For Exercises 1–3, find each sum. Do not use a calculator.

1. $2131 + 3424$

2. $7654 + 2222$

3. $1571 + 5212$

4. The plans for a garden show the dimensions as 8 yards long and 5 yards wide. The actual garden is 5 feet longer and 2 feet narrower than the plans show. Find the actual length and width of the garden. Give your answers in yards and in feet.

5. Find the sum $\frac{1}{2} + \frac{1}{4} + \frac{1}{5} + \frac{1}{6}$ without a calculator.

For Exercises 6–8, evaluate the expression. Do not use a calculator.

6. $36 \cdot \left(\frac{1}{2} + \frac{1}{3} + \frac{1}{4} + \frac{1}{6} \right)$

7. $100 \cdot \left(\frac{1}{2} + \frac{1}{5} + \frac{1}{20} + \frac{1}{25} \right)$

8. $30 \cdot \left(\frac{1}{2} + \frac{1}{3} + \frac{1}{5} + \frac{1}{6} \right)$

For Exercises 9–12, find three distinct fractions having a sum that equals each number given.

9. 2

10. -4

11. $\frac{1}{2}$

12. 0

For Exercises 13–15, find each sum. Write the result in lowest terms.

13. $\frac{1}{100} + \frac{1}{200} + \frac{1}{300} + \frac{1}{600}$

14. $\frac{1}{15} + \frac{1}{30} + \frac{1}{45} + \frac{1}{90}$

15. $\frac{1}{11} + \frac{1}{22} + \frac{1}{33} + \frac{1}{66}$

16. Describe the pattern that you used to find the results for Exercises 13–15.

Additional Practice

1. a. How can you find the number of feet in 1 million inches?

   b. Describe how to use the result from part (a) to find the number of miles in 1 million inches. Calculate the number of miles in 1 million inches. Round to the nearest mile.

For Exercises 2–5, use an expansion box to find each product.

2. 537×8

3. 6×709

4. 2357×7

5. $14{,}012 \times 3$

For Exercises 6–9, find each product. Do not use a calculator.

6. 23×201

7. 25×201

8. 37×201

9. 42×201

10. Describe the pattern that you used to find each product in Exercises 6–9.

11. How many 5's are in 245?

12. How many $\frac{1}{2}$'s are in 31?

13. How many $\frac{1}{6}$'s are in $\frac{45}{2}$?

14. A student said, "To reduce the fraction $\frac{16}{64}$, just erase the common digit 6 and you get $\frac{1}{4}$." Does this method work to reduce $\frac{24}{48}$, $\frac{12}{24}$, or $\frac{13}{39}$? Explain.

15. Multiple Choice Which fraction gives a correct reduced result if you use the method in Exercise 14?

  A. $\frac{16}{21}$ **B.** $\frac{23}{36}$ **C.** $\frac{14}{51}$ **D.** $\frac{19}{95}$

For Exercises 16–18, write each fraction in lowest terms.

16. $\dfrac{\frac{4}{7}}{\frac{8}{7}}$

17. $\dfrac{\frac{13}{5}}{\frac{25}{5}}$

18. $\dfrac{\frac{105}{301}}{\frac{106}{301}}$

Additional Practice

1. Suppose a pepperoni pizza should bake 7 minutes longer than a plain pizza.
   a. If a small plain pizza should bake for 12 minutes, how long should you bake a small pepperoni pizza?
   b. If a large plain pizza should bake for m minutes, how long should you bake a large pepperoni pizza?

2. Match each expression below to a set of steps (a)–(c).
      I. $-3(x - 4)$ **II.** $-3x - 4$ **III.** $4(x - 3)$

   a. Choose any number.   **b.** Choose any number.
       Subtract 3.   Subtract 4.
       Multiply by 4.   Multiply by -3.
   c. Choose any number.
       Multiply by -3.
       Subtract 4.

3. Keith writes an expression using the following steps.
   - Start with x.
   - Multiply by -2.
   - Subtract 7.
   - Subtract 12.

   He writes the final expression $-2(x - 7) - 12$. Explain what he did wrong. Then find the correct expression.

4. Spiro says, "Choose a number. Add 5. Multiply by -4. Subtract 3."
   For each starting number given, what is your ending number?
     a. -3 **b.** 10   **c.** m **d.** 0

5. Evaluate $\dfrac{3x + 5x - 6x + 2x}{x}$ for each value of x.
     a. 6   **b.** 22   **c.** -13 **d.** 4

6. You have a tube that can be stretched or compressed. As you change the length of the tube, the density d of the gas inside the tube and the volume V change according to the expression $d = \dfrac{100}{V}$. Find the density of the gas for each volume given in cubic units.
     a. 1   **b.** 25   **c.** 200

7. Kathy evaluates the expression $3x - 2$ for $x = 5$ and $x = 2$. When $x = 5$, she gets $3x - 2 = 3 \cdot (5 - 2) = 3 \cdot 3 = 9$. When $x = 2$, she gets $3x - 2 = 3 \cdot (2 - 2) = 3 \cdot 0 = 0$.
   a. What does Kathy do wrong?
   b. For $x = 5$ and for $x = 2$, what is the correct evaluation of $3x - 2$?

Additional Practice

1. Use the basic rules of arithmetic and what you know about like terms. Decide which expressions equal the expression $3m - 5n$. If an expression does not equal $3m - 5n$, explain why it does not.
   a. $3(m - n) - 4n$ **b.** $(3m)(-5n)$ **c.** $(2m - 7n) + (m + 2n)$

2. The lengths and widths of three rectangles are given below. For each rectangle, find an expression for the area and an expression for the perimeter.
   a. length: $12x - 7$ width: 5
   b. length: 13   width: $-3x - 4$
   c. length: $5 + 7x$ width: 8

3. Evaluate the expression $5(2x - 7) - 3(3x - 10) + 4$ for each x value.
   a. 4   **b.** -5 **c.** $\frac{1}{10}$ **d.** 0
   e. Simplify the expression.

4. Evaluate the expression $\frac{n(n + 1)}{2}$ for each n value.
   a. 7   **b.** 8   **c.** 9   **d.** 10
   e. Explain why $\frac{n(n + 1)}{2}$ is always a whole number if n is a whole number.

5. The binary operation $\boxdot$ is defined by the rule $a \boxdot b = \frac{2ab}{a + b}$.
   a. Explain how to find $5 \boxdot 3 = 3.75$.
   b. Evaluate $10 \boxdot 3$.
   c. Is $\boxdot$ commutative? That is, does $\boxdot$ have the any-order property?

6. Simplify.
   a. $3(y + 5) + 4(y + 5)$ **b.** $3(y + 5) + 4(y + 5) - 6(y + 5)$
   c. Evaluate each simplified expression for $y = -5$. What is the pattern in your results? Explain.

7. Here is one of Maya the Magnificent's number tricks.
   • Choose a number.
   • Subtract 6.
   • Multiply by 5.
   • Add 100.
   • Multiply by 2.
   • Subtract 20.
   • Divide by 10.

   Maya says, "I can get your starting number from your ending number in one step!"
   a. Let the starting number equal m. Write the result after each step. Simplify each expression after each step.
   b. Explain how Maya can get the starting number from any ending number in one step.

Additional Practice

1. Write each algebraic expression as a statement of an operation. If the operation is reversible, describe the operation that reverses it.

   a. $-5x - 7$

   b. $\dfrac{x + 6}{3}$

   c. $15 - 4x$

2. Michelle says, "I take a number, multiply by 5, and then subtract 2. My final result is -17." What is Michelle's starting number?

3. Describe how you can use backtracking to solve the equation $\dfrac{x - 1017}{528} = 203$. Describe the steps you perform without solving the equation.

4. For each operation, find a number that produces itself as the output.
   a. Add 2 to your number and then divide by 2.
   b. Multiply your number by 5 and then add 4.

Use backtracking to find the solution of each equation in Exercises 5–7.

5. $12 - 3w = 27$

6. $\dfrac{x}{15} = -6$

7. $5z - 13 = 7$

8. The equation $4m + 3n = 36$ gives a relationship between the variables m and n.
   a. If the value of m is 8, find the value of n.
   b. If the value of n is 2, find the value of m.
   c. Complete the table relating m and n for different values of m.

m	n
0	
1	
2	
3	
4	
5	
6	

For Exercises 9–11, solve each equation using backtracking.

9. $-3x + 15 = 4$

10. $12 + 11x = 9$

11. $4 - 3x = 15$

Additional Practice

Solve each equation.

1. $5m + 6 = m + 18$

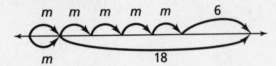

2. $5n + 7 = 3n + 15$

3. $4x = -44$

4. $6y - 7 = 23$

5. $60 = -15z$

6. $2z + 3 = 17$

7. $2(z - 1) + 3 = 17$

8. $2(1 - 5z) + 3 = 17$

9. $6x + 3 = 13 + x$

10. $7x + 3 = 13 + x$

11. $8x + 3 = 13 + x$

12. Which steps are the same for solving each of the equations in Exercises 9–11? Which steps are different?

13. Suppose that you teach a robot to do your algebra homework. Give the steps for solving the equation $17x - 23 = 32x + 48$. Show the result of each step.

Solve each equation in Exercises 14–15.

14. $11s + 7 = 8s - 17$

15. $17t - 26 = 11t + 51$

16. Describe *one* basic move you can use to transform the equation $3x - 17 = 20$ into each equation.

   a. $3x - 10 = 27$

   b. $3x - 30 = 7$

   c. $x - 17 = 20 - 2x$

   d. $3x = 37$

   e. $3x - 37 = 0$

   f. $x - \frac{17}{3} = \frac{20}{3}$

17. Solve each equation in Exercise 16 for x. Explain your results.

18. Solve each equation.

   a. $6x - 4 = 17 - x$

   b. $(6x - 4) - 5 = (17 - x) - 5$

   c. $(6x - 4) + 8 = (17 - x) + 8$

   d. What do these equations have in common? Explain.

Additional Practice

Solve each equation.

1. $2(n + 1) + 1 = (n - 5) + (n - 2)$

2. $3(n - 1) - 2 = 4(n - 4) - (n - 11)$

3. $3(n + 2) + 4n = 4(n + 2) + 4$

4. $7(2n - 3) = 5(3n - 4)$

5. $5(1 - n) + 3n = 3(n - 1) - 5n$

6. $4(n + 1) + (n + 3) = 5(n + 1) + 2$

7. $7 = 6x - 5$

8. $7 = 6(x + 1) - 5$

9. $6(x - 3) - 5 = 7$

10. $7 = 6(x + 4) - 5$

11. $7 = 6(1 - 2y) - 5$

12. $7 = 6(2z + 3) - 5$

13. Explain how you can use the basic moves of algebra to transform the equation $5x - 3y = 12$ into each of the following equations.

  a. $0 = 12 - 5x + 3y$ **b.** $5x = 3y + 12$ **c.** $x = \frac{3y}{5} + \frac{12}{5}$

Solve each equation.

14. $21 = 5(x + 3)$

15. $8(k + 3) = 5(k - 3)$

16. $7(m + 3) - 8 = 6$

17. $-(n - 11) = -3$

18. $-(p + 17) = 5(p - 3)$

19. $-15 = -3(4t - 3)$

20. $7(3a + 4) = -35$

21. $-(b - 17) = -2$

22. $33 = -11(c - 6)$

23. $-(-4 + s) = -\frac{1}{3}(12s - 21)$

24. $-(w - \frac{3}{5}) = 2w$

Additional Practice

1. Last month, Katie started training for the swim team. She swam 20 laps every day for 18 training days. This month, Katie wants to swim 215 more laps than last month. She will swim 3 more laps per training day and add more training days to her monthly schedule.
   a. If Katie adds 5 training days to her schedule this month, will she swim 215 more laps?
   b. If Katie adds 10 training days to her schedule this month, will she swim 215 more laps?
   c. If Katie adds 6 training days to her schedule this month, will she swim 215 more laps?
   d. Use the guess-check-generalize method to build an equation for finding the number of additional training days she needs to swim 215 more laps.
   e. Solve your equation.

2. On a trip, a family drives one third of the way on the first day. After driving 200 miles on the second day, they are seven ninths of the way to their destination. How many miles is their trip?

3. Last year, the price of a certain computer was $150 more than it is now. This year's price is $\frac{3}{4}$ of last year's price. How much does the computer cost this year?

4. Jan participates in a bowling tournament. Her average score for 11 games is 204. Without her lowest score, her average is 207. What is Jan's lowest score?

5. a. At the start of the school year, sportswriters say that your school's football team has a 40% chance of being the best team in the league. What is the probability that your team will lead the league?
   b. What is the probability that your team will not lead the league?
   c. Suppose the sportswriters say that the probability of your team coming in first or second is w. Find the probability that your team will not come in first or second, in terms of w.

6. If Tom's baby sister adds 5 pounds to her weight, she will be 25% heavier than she is now. How much does she weigh now?

7. During a cat food sale, a pet store sells 220 cans of cat food. At the end of the sale, the store has 80% of the original number of cans of cat food. How many cans of cat food are left?

8. Victor tried to solve the equation $2(5 - 3x) = -5(3x + 7)$.
   a. Show that Victor found the incorrect result.
   b. Explain what Victor did wrong.
   c. Solve the equation correctly.

$$2(5 - 3x) = -5(3x + 7)$$
$$10 - 6x = -15x - 35$$
$$10 - 6x + 15x = -15x - 35 + 15x$$
$$10 - 9x = -35$$
$$-9x = -35 - 10$$
$$-9x = -45$$
$$x = 5$$

CME Project • *Algebra 1 Teaching Resources*

Additional Practice

1. Solve the equation $3a - 2b + 7 = 4a - 3b + 10$ for a. Then solve the equation for b.

2. The equation $7x - 3y = 42$ relates x and y.
   a. Suppose x is 4 and y is 25. Do these values make the equation true? Explain.
   b. Suppose x is 9. Find a value of y that makes the equation true.
   c. Find three pairs of points (x, y) that make the equation true.

3. You can find the perimeter of a rectangle if you subtract the width from the length, add 7 inches, and multiply the result by 4.
   a. If the rectangle's length is ℓ and its width is w, what is its perimeter?
   b. Explain why the equation $2\ell + 2w = 4(\ell - w + 7)$ is true for the rectangle.
   c. Solve the equation in part (b) for the variable ℓ.
   d. If the rectangle's width is 8 inches, what is the length? What is its perimeter?

4. A shoe store makes $2880 during a one-day sale. Men's shoes cost $24 per pair and women's shoes cost $18 per pair. Let m equal the number of pairs of men's shoes and w equal the number of pairs of women's shoes. The equation $24m + 18w = 2880$ describes the store's income for the sale.
   a. If the store sold 30 pairs of men's shoes during the sale, how many pairs of women's shoes were sold?
   b. Can the store have sold exactly 150 pairs of women's shoes during the sale? Explain.
   c. The store sold one more pair of men's shoes than women's shoes during the sale. How many pairs of each were sold?

5. Consider the equation $4x + 7y = 56$.
   a. Solve for y. Write the equation in the form $y = $ an expression.
   b. Solve for x.

6. Consider the equation $5x + 7y = 29$.
   a. Solve for y.
   b. Solve for x.

Additional Practice

1. Describe how a point's location changes after you add a negative value to the y-coordinate of an ordered pair and leave the x-coordinate the same.

2. How can you change the coordinates of a point so that you shift the point to the right?

3. Apply each transformation to the point $P(-4, 6)$. Then describe how the position of P changes with each transformation given.
   a. Change the sign of its y-coordinate, but keep the sign of the x-coordinate the same.
   b. Change the sign of its x-coordinate, but keep the sign of the y-coordinate the same.
   c. Change the signs of both coordinates.

4. Draw the square with corners $M(0, 0)$, $A(2, 0)$, $T(2, 2)$, and $H(0, 2)$. Transform each point using the rule given. Then graph the new shape on the same coordinate plane. Describe the effect of the transformation on each point and on the square.
   a. $(x, y) \mapsto (x, -2y)$
   b. $(x, y) \mapsto (2y, -2x)$

5. Is it possible for a line to pass through exactly two quadrants? Explain.

6. Is it possible for a line to pass through no quadrants? Explain.

For Exercises 7–10, apply the transformation to each shape given. Draw a sketch for each transformation. Then describe how the transformation changes each shape.

7. $(x, y) \mapsto (x + 3, y + 4)$; a triangle with corners $(-3, 5)$, $(0, 7)$, and $(2, 1)$

8. $(x, y) \mapsto (x, y - 4)$; a rectangle with corners $(1, 1)$, $(1, 3)$, $(2, 3)$, and $(2, 1)$

9. $(x, y) \mapsto (2x, 3y)$; a square with corners $(0, 0)$, $(4, 0)$, $(4, 4)$, and $(0, 4)$

10. $(x, y) \mapsto (-y, -2x)$; a triangle with corners $(0, 0)$, $(4, 0)$, and $(4, 4)$

Additional Practice

1. Write a sentence about distance that restates the equation given. Then find two numbers that make the equation true.

   a. $|x - 11| = 5$ **b.** $|x + 3| = 12$ **c.** $|x - 4| < 3$

2. Find the distance between each pair of points.

   a. $(-3, 7)$ and $(-3, -3)$ **b.** $(5, -12)$ and $(0, 0)$ **c.** the origin and $(8, 15)$

3. Find an equation using absolute values that has the solutions given.

   a. two solutions, -17 and 17 **b.** two solutions, 7 and 15

   c. one solution, 6 **d.** two solutions, -5 and -11

   e. two solutions, -2 and 8 **f.** no solution

4. Find the solutions to each equation.

   a. $|x| = 15$ **b.** $|3x| = 15$ **c.** $|10x| = 15$ **d.** $|300x| = 15$

   e. What is the pattern to the solutions?

5. Write a sentence that can explain this graph when the axes have the following labels.

Horizontal Axis	Vertical Axis
a. Time (minutes)	Number of Pages Read
b. Length (ft)	Wingspan (ft)

   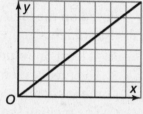

6. Monica's exercise routine includes stretching, walking, and jogging. This graph illustrates her exercise routine.

   a. Between which two points is Monica stretching? Explain.

   b. Between which two points is Monica walking? Explain.

   c. Between which two points is Monica jogging? Explain.

   Monica's Exercise Routine

   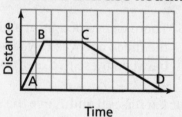

7. Make a graph that illustrates each situation by graphing distance against time.

   a. For exercise, Sam walks and Beth jogs. Sam walks at a steady pace for 10 minutes. Beth waits for 3 minutes after Sam starts. She jogs, rests in place for 1 minute, jogs again, and catches up to Sam at the end of the 10 minutes.

   b. Cathy leaves her house and walks toward a park. Two minutes later, Dave starts walking from the park toward Cathy's house. Four minutes later, they meet.

Additional Practice

1. Find the median of these five numbers.

   3.15×10^5 6.0×10^8 750 1.003×10^{18} 17

2. Describe how you can obtain each data set below from the data set {52, 51, 47, 49, 41}. Then describe how the mean and median change for each new set.
   a. {104, 102, 94, 98, 82}   b. {50, 49, 45, 47, 39}

3. Find the mean of each pair of numbers. Graph the mean on a number line.
   a. 12 and 20   b. −8 and 10
   c. −25 and −19   d. 17 and 18
   e. Describe the position of the mean in terms of the two points.

4. **Multiple Choice** Each of 30 students takes a math exam. The table shows the results of the exam.

   Based on the table, which statement about the students' scores is true?

   A. At least one student scored exactly 90.
   B. The median score is greater than the mean score.
   C. The median score is between 85 and 94.
   D. 9% of the students score between 95 and 100.

   Math Exam Scores

Score Range	Number of Students
70–78	2
79–84	8
85–94	11
95–100	9

5. There were 9 people at a birthday party. The median age was 3 years and the mean age was 19 years. What could account for such a wide difference between these two measures?

For Exercises 6 and 7, use the stem-and-leaf display that shows the high temperature in 40 cities on one day.

6. **Multiple Choice** Which percent of the cities had a high temperature less than 58°F?
   A. 18%   B. 42%
   C. 45%   D. 58%

High Temperatures in 40 Cities (°F)

4	1 1 3 3 4 5 5 6 6 6 7 8
5	2 2 2 6 7 7 9 9
6	2 3 3 7 7 8 9 9
7	0 0 1 1 2 3 5 7 7 7 7 8

7. a. How many cities had a high temperature of 70°F or greater?
   b. Compare the number of cities that had a high temperature greater than 60°F with the number of cities that had a high temperature less than 60°F.
   c. Which high temperature was the same for 4 cities?
   d. Which high temperature was the same for 3 cities?

Name _____ Class _____ Date _____

Additional Practice

1. Each of two data sets, Set A and Set B, has the same interquartile range, the same minimum value, and the same maximum value.
  a. Draw a possible paired box-and-whisker plot for Set A and Set B.
  b. Is it possible for the third quartile of Set A to be equal to the first quartile of Set B? Explain.

2. Multiple Choice The box-and-whisker plot shows the average bowling scores of 40 members of a bowling league.

Based on the box-and-whisker plot, which statement must be true?

  A. More bowlers have average scores between 180 and 200 than average scores between 230 and 240.
  B. The range of bowlers' average scores is 60.
  C. The mean of the average scores is 220.
  D. The lowest average score is 200.

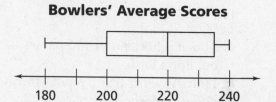

Bowlers' Average Scores

180   200   220   240

3. A car dealership reported two five-number summaries for the selling prices of the last 28 new cars and last 28 used cars sold.

Make a paired box-and-whisker plot for the new and used car selling prices. Describe what the plot shows about the data sets.

	New Cars	Used Cars
Minimum	$12,000	$4,000
First Quartile	$18,000	$5,500
Median	$26,000	$12,000
Third Quartile	$32,000	$22,000
Maximum	$45,000	$30,000

4. Each week during track season, athletes run a half-mile race. Here is a table of the mean times for weeks 1 through 10.

Week	1	2	3	4	5	6	7	8	9	10
Time (s)	154	151	148	146	141	135	131	128	124	122

  a. Make a scatter plot. Show the weeks from 1 to 10 on the horizontal axis. Show time on the vertical axis.
  b. Based on the scatter plot, guess the average time for week 17.

5. At five schools, the teachers timed the evacuation of their students during two fire drills. The table shows the results.
  a. Make a scatter plot.
  b. Is there a trend to the data?
  c. Are there any outliers?

School	Week 1 (min)	Week 4 (min)
A	8.5	5.4
B	7.1	4.5
C	8.0	4.8
D	9.5	3.2
E	9.2	6.1

Name _____ Class _____ Date _____

Additional Practice

1. **a.** Name and plot six points that are on the graph of $x = -3$.
   b. Describe the graph of $x = -3$. Draw the graph.

2. The graph of the equation $x = y^2$ is a sideways parabola.
   a. Determine whether $(5, 25)$, $(25, 5)$, $(0, 1)$, and $(1, -1)$ are on the graph.
   b. Find four more points that are on the graph.

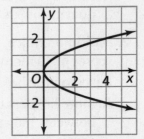

3. Let $Q = (3, -5)$.
   a. Line h is horizontal and passes through Q. Write an equation for h.
   b. Line v is vertical and passes through Q. Write an equation for v.

4. Use your equations from Exercise 3 to determine whether each of the following points is on h, v, neither h nor v, or on both h and v.
   a. $(0, 0)$ **b.** $(3, 3)$ **c.** $(-5, -5)$ **d.** $(3, -5)$ **e.** $(-3, 5)$

5. Line a is vertical and passes through $(2, -3)$. Line b is horizontal and passes through $(-1, -4)$.
   a. Find four points on a.
   b. Find four points on b.
   c. Write a point-tester equation for a.
   d. Write a point-tester equation for b.
   e. Graph a and b on the same coordinate plane. Label both lines and their point of intersection.

6. **a.** Find five points that satisfy the equation $3x - 4y = 36$.
   b. Find five points that do not satisfy the equation $3x - 4y = 36$.

7. Graph each equation on the same coordinate plane. Label each equation on the graph.
   a. $y = -x$ **b.** $y + 1 = -x$ **c.** $y + 2 = -x$
   d. $y + 3 = -x$ **e.** $y + 4 = -x$ **f.** $y + 5 = -x$
   g. How do the equations change?
   h. How does the change affect the graphs?
   i. Without plotting any points, describe the graph of $y + 10 = -x$.

Name _____ Class _____ Date _____

Additional Practice

1. These four equations may look different, but three of them have the same graph. Which graph is different?

   A. $y - 5 = \frac{5}{3}(x - 6)$ **B.** $3y - 5x = 15$

   C. $5x - 3y = 15$ **D.** $y = \frac{5}{3}x - 5$

2. Match each equation with a graph. Explain each choice.

   I. $y = -(x + 2)^2$ **II.** $-x + y = -2$ **III.** $y = -5$ **IV.** $x = 5$

   a. 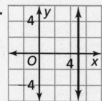   **b.** 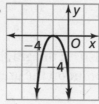   **c.** 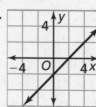   **d.**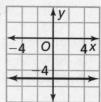

3. Graph each equation.

   a. $(y - 5) = x$ **b.** $(y - 3) = x + 1$ **c.** $(y - 3) = x - 1$

4. **a.** Does the graph of the equation $y = -2x + 7$ intersect the graph of the equation $y = -2x + 2$? Explain.

   b. Describe the result you find when you solve the equation $-2x + 7 = -2x + 2$.

5. Find the equations of two lines that are neither vertical nor horizontal, and which intersect at the point $(8, -4)$. Show that the point $(8, -4)$ makes both equations true.

6. Look at the graphs of $x^2 + y^2 = 4$ and $x + y = 2$.
   a. Match each graph with its equation.
   b. Use the graphs to estimate the points where the graphs intersect. Use the equations to show that your guesses are correct or to find better guesses.

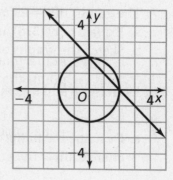

7. Find the intersection of the graph $x = -3$ with the graph of each equation.
   a. $y = 0$ **b.** $y = 1$ **c.** $y = 2$ **d.** $y = 3$
   e. $y = 4$ **f.** $y = 5$ **g.** $y = 6$ **h.** $y = 7$
   i. $y = 8$ **j.** $y = 9$
   k. What is the pattern of the graphs? Explain.

Name _____ Class _____ Date _____

Additional Practice

1. Decide whether each point is on the graph of $y = -8x$.
  a. $(4, -2)$ **b.** $(-2, 4)$ **c.** $(-1, 8)$

  d. $(1, -8)$ **e.** $(0, 0)$ **f.** $(16, -\frac{1}{2})$

2. Decide whether each point in Exercise 1 is on the graph of $xy = -8$.

3. a. Graph $y = -8x$ and $xy = -8$ on the same coordinate plane.
  b. How many times do the graphs intersect? What are the points of intersection?

4. Suppose (p, q) is on the graph of $xy = 48$.
  a. Show that $(-p, -q)$ and $(-q, -p)$ are also on the graph.
  b. Find the missing coordinates of each point on the graph.

   $(4, \square)$ $(\frac{1}{2}p, \square)$ $(5q, \square)$

5. A shipping store sells four boxes for a total of $9.00.
  a. How much do you pay for 20 boxes?
  b. How much do you pay for one box if each box costs the same amount?
  c. Write a rule relating the number b of boxes to the total cost c.

6. The cost of downloading songs varies directly with the number of songs that you download. Suppose one song costs $2.75 to download.
  a. Find the number of songs you can download for $22.00.
  b. What is the cost to download 11 songs?
  c. What is the cost to download 22 songs?
  d. Draw a graph of the total cost against the number of downloaded songs.
  e. Find an equation relating the total cost c to the number of downloaded songs s.

7. The graphs of $y = 2x$ and $xy = 18$ intersect at two points.
  a. Explain why $(3, 6)$ and $(-3, -6)$ are intersection points.
  b. Sketch the graphs on graph paper. Show the points of the intersection.

For Exercises 8 and 9, graph each equation on the same coordinate plane.

8. a. $y = -x$ **b.** $y = -2x$ **c.** $y = -3x$ **d.** $y = -4x$
  e. Describe the pattern. How do the equations change? How does this change affect the graphs?

9. a. $y = -x$ **b.** $y = -\frac{1}{2}x$ **c.** $y = -\frac{1}{3}x$ **d.** $y = -\frac{1}{4}x$
  e. Describe the pattern. How do the equations change? How does this change affect the graphs?

Name _____ Class _____ Date _____

Additional Practice

1. Sketch a graph of each equation. What are the possible values of x and y?

   a. $y = \sqrt{x + 4}$ **b.** $y = \sqrt{-2x}$

2. **Multiple Choice** Choose the rule that shows the relationship between x and y in the table.

   A. $y = -2x + 2$ **B.** $y = 2x$ **C.** $y = \sqrt{x}$ **D.** $y = 2x^2$

x	y
−2	8
−1	2
0	0
1	2
2	8
3	18
4	32

3. Find the number of points of intersection for the graph of each pair of equations.

   a. $y = |x|$ and $y = 5$ **b.** $y = |x|$ and $x = 3$

   c. $y = x^2$ and $y = \frac{1}{x}$ **d.** $y = x^3$ and $y = x + 3$

   e. $y = \frac{1}{x}$ and $y = x$ **f.** $y = x^3$ and $y = -x^2$

4. Sketch the graph of each equation.

   a. $y = (x - 1)^2$ **b.** $(y + 2) = (x + 1)^2$ **c.** $(y + 2) = x^3$

   d. $(y + 2) = (x - 3)^3$ **e.** $y = \sqrt{x - 5}$ **f.** $y = \sqrt{x + 5}$

   g. How are the graphs in parts (a)–(f) related to the basic graphs?

5. Transform each equation using each rule given. Write the resulting equation and sketch its graph.

   a. $y = x^2$, $(x, y) \mapsto (x - 3, y)$

   b. $y = x^2$, $(x, y) \mapsto (x, y + 3)$

   c. $y = |x|$, $(x, y) \mapsto (x - 3, y + 4)$

6. Sketch the graph of each equation on the same coordinate plane.

   a. $(y + 3) = (x - 1)^2$ **b.** $(y + 3) = (x - 1)^3$ **c.** $(y + 3) = (x - 1)$

7. The graph of the equation $(y + 5) = (x + 2)^2 + M$ passes through the point $(1, 3)$. Find the value of M.

8. Use this graph of $x^2 - xy + y^2 = 27$ to describe the graph of $(x - 2)^2 - (x - 2)(y + 1) + (y + 1)^2 = 27$. Then sketch the new graph.

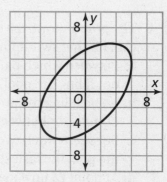

9. Sketch the graph of each pair of equations. Describe the relationship between the graphs of each pair of equations.

   a. $y = \frac{2}{3}x$ and $(y - 2) = \frac{2}{3}(x - 3)$

   b. $y = -2(x - 4)$ and $(y + 2) = -2(x - 5)$

10. Using the graphs you drew in Exercise 9, find an ordered pair (x, y) that makes all the equations in 9a and 9b true.

Name _____ Class _____ Date _____

Additional Practice

1. Find the slope of the line between each pair of points.
  a. $(-3, 5)$ and $(0, 0)$
  b. $(6, 2)$ and $(-3, 5)$

  c. $(3, 5)$ and $(-6, 2)$
  d. $\left(\frac{2}{3}, -7\right)$ and $\left(\frac{1}{3}, -7\right)$

  e. $\left(-\frac{3}{4}, -5\right)$ and $\left(-\frac{3}{4}, 11\right)$
  f. $(5, 8)$ and $(-5, -8)$

2. Given $P(-2, 6)$ and $O(0, 0)$, find a point Q that makes the following true.
  a. $m(P, Q) = 4$
  b. $m(P, Q) = -4$

  c. $m(P, Q) = m(O, Q)$
  d. $m(P, Q) = -\frac{1}{4}$

  e. $m(O, Q) = -\frac{2}{3}$
  f. $m(P, Q) = 0$

  g. $m(P, Q) = -\frac{5}{12}$ and the distance between points P and Q is 13.

3. How can you describe the relative positions of P and Q in the following situations?
  a. $m(P, Q) = 0$
  b. $m(P, Q) < 0$
  c. $m(P, Q) > 0$
  d. $m(P, Q)$ does not exist.

4. a. Graph the points $M(-3, -5)$ and $N(15, 1)$. Draw line $\overleftrightarrow{MN}$.
  b. What is $m(M, N)$?
  c. Choose another point R on $\overleftrightarrow{MN}$. Calculate $m(M, R)$ and $m(N, R)$.

5. Gail has a swimming pool that holds 15,000 gallons of water. How long does it take to fill the pool using the following water hoses?
  a. a garden hose that provides 25 gallons per minute
  b. a fire hose that provides 200 gallons per minute
  c. both hoses at the same time

6. The graph shows the amount of water as Gail fills her swimming pool.
  a. Between which pair of points is Gail not filling the pool?
  b. Is she filling the pool slower between O and A, or between B and C?
  c. Between which two points is she filling the pool the fastest?
  d. At point D, how many gallons are in the pool? How many hours did it take? What average rate would give the same result?

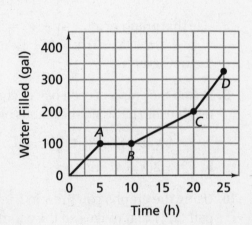

Name _____ Class _____ Date _____

Additional Practice

Lesson 4.4

1. Which three points lie on the same line? Explain.

   $P(-9, 4)$ $Q(6, 2)$ $R(-3, -4)$ $S(9, 4)$

2. Describe a point-tester to determine whether a point is on the line that contains $(-3, 5)$ and $(6, -7)$.

3. Find three points on the graph of each equation. Are they collinear?

   a. $y - 2 = -3(x - 5)$ **b.** $y = \frac{1}{3}x + 4$

   c. $4x - 2y = 10$ **d.** $y + 3 = -\frac{1}{2}(x + 8)$

   e. $y = \frac{1}{3x}$ **f.** $y = -2x^2$

4. Suppose t is the line that contains the points $P(-6, -1)$ and $Q(3, 5)$. Which of the following points are on t? Explain.

   a. $(6, 6)$ **b.** $(6, 7)$ **c.** $(6, 8)$

   d. $\left(1, \frac{8}{3}\right)$ **e.** $\left(1, \frac{10}{3}\right)$ **f.** $\left(1, \frac{11}{3}\right)$

   g. $\left(-4, \frac{1}{2}\right)$ **h.** $\left(-4, \frac{1}{3}\right)$ **i.** $\left(-4, \frac{1}{4}\right)$

5. **Multiple Choice** Which equation describes the relationship between x and y in the table?

   A. $x + y = 9$ **B.** $2x - 3y = 17$
   C. $-2x - 7y = 53$ **D.** $3x - 2y = 8$

x	y
-2	-7
-1	$-5\frac{1}{2}$
1	$-2\frac{1}{2}$
2	-1
3	$\frac{1}{2}$

For Exercises 6 and 7, points X, Y, and Z are collinear. Is point W collinear with points X, Y, and Z? Look for a pattern.

6. **a.** $X(5, 5)$, $Y(7, 7)$, $Z(9, 9)$, $W(17, 17)$
   b. $X(-2, -2)$, $Y(-3, -3)$, $Z(-10, -10)$, $W(5, -5)$
   c. $X(1, -1)$, $Y(3, -3)$, $Z(6, -6)$, $W(10, 10)$
   d. $X(-2, 2)$, $Y(-5, 5)$, $Z(-11, 11)$, $W(-25, 25)$
   e. Describe a pattern.

7. **a.** $X(2, 5)$, $Y(4, 7)$, $Z(8, 11)$, $W(15, 18)$
   b. $X(-5, -2)$, $Y(-1, 2)$, $Z(0, 3)$, $W(20, 30)$
   c. $X(5, -5)$, $Y(11, 1)$, $Z(15, 5)$, $W(29, 19)$
   d. $X(-3, -13)$, $Y(-6, -16)$, $Z(-8, -18)$, $W(-29, -19)$
   e. Describe a pattern.

CME Project • *Algebra 1 Teaching Resources*

Additional Practice

1. For each equation, do the following.
   - Decide whether the graph is a line. Explain.
   - If the equation represents a line, find the slope and the points where the line crosses the x- and y-axes.

   a. $x^2 + y^2 = 16$ **b.** $5x + 4y = 80$ **c.** $y - 7 = \frac{4}{5}(x + 10)$

   d. $y = -\frac{1}{4}x - 10$ **e.** $xy = -4$ **f.** $2x - 3y = 18$

2. Prove that the slope between any two points on the line $5x + y = 7$ is -5.

3. Find the slope of each line with the given description or equation.

   a. contains $(-2, 15)$ and $(-6, 39)$ **b.** $y = -\frac{5}{6}x + 11$

   c. $2.718x - 2.718y = 11$ **d.** $y - 7 = \frac{5}{13}(x - 11)$

   e. $y - 1.618 = \frac{5}{13}(x + 1.414)$

   f. contains the origin and is parallel to the line in part (c)

4. Keisuke can type at a rate of 37 words per minute.
   a. How many words can he type in 8 minutes?
   b. How many words can he type in 13 minutes?
   c. **Multiple Choice** Let m be the number of minutes that Keisuke types. Let w be the number of words that he types. Which equation represents the relationship between m and w?
   A. $m = w + 37$ **B.** $w = m + 37$
   C. $m = 37w$ **D.** $w = 37m$

5. **Multiple Choice** What is the slope of the line with the equation $3x - 8y = 24$?

   A. $-\frac{8}{3}$ **B.** $-\frac{3}{8}$ **C.** $\frac{3}{8}$ **D.** $\frac{8}{3}$

6. Find an equation of the line that contains $(7, -6)$ and has a slope of -2. Then find another point on the line. Can you find a point that is on the line but does not satisfy your equation?

7. Sketch each pair of equations. Do the lines intersect?
   a. $y + 5 = 3(x - 8)$ and $y + 5 = -4(x - 8)$

   b. $y - 10 = x + 5$ and $y - 10 = -4(x + 5)$

   c. $y + \frac{15}{23} = \frac{2}{3}\left(x + \frac{7}{23}\right)$ and $y + \frac{15}{23} = \frac{1}{3}\left(x + \frac{7}{23}\right)$

   d. What pattern do you notice in the line intersections?

Name _____ Class _____ Date _____

Additional Practice

Lessons 4.7 and 4.8

1. Write an equation for each line that contains the given point and that has the given slope m.

   a. $(5, -2)$; $m = -2$ **b.** $(-3, 4)$; $m = \frac{1}{3}$

   c. $(8, -2)$; $m = -\frac{2}{3}$ **d.** $(-4, -7)$; $m = -\frac{2}{5}$

   e. $(12, 7)$; $m = 0$ **f.** $(-8, -11)$; slope is undefined

2. Graph each equation.

   a. $y + 5 = -(x + 3)$ **b.** $y + \frac{2}{3} = -\frac{3}{2}\left(x - \frac{1}{3}\right)$ **c.** $y = 2x + 4$

   d. $y = -\frac{3}{5}x + \frac{5}{2}$ **e.** $y = \frac{7}{3}x - 2$ **f.** $y = -\frac{1}{2}(x + 2) + 3$

3. Mara does yard work for $8 per hour. She buys a rake and other tools for $35.

   a. **Multiple Choice** Which equation represents the relationship between the total amount of money p that Mara makes and the number of hours h she works?

      A. $p = 8h - 35$ **B.** $p = 8h + 35$ **C.** $h = 8p - 35$ **D.** $h = 8p + 35$

   b. How many hours must Mara work to make a total profit of $85?

4. The distance-time graphs show Kristin's and Vicky's run around a track.

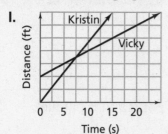 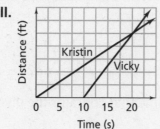 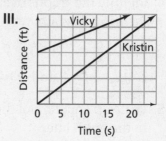

   a. Which graphs show Kristin and Vicky starting at the same time?

   b. Which graphs show Kristin and Vicky starting at different times? Which runner starts first?

   c. Who is running faster in graph I? In graph II?

   d. Write equations for the two lines in graph II if Vicky overtakes Kristin at the point (20, 300).

5. Paul and Rob often run half-mile races. Paul's best time in the race is $3\frac{1}{2}$ minutes. Rob's best time is $2\frac{3}{4}$ minutes.

   a. In yesterday's race, Paul had a 30-second head start. Assume that both matched the speed of their best times. Sketch a distance-time graph that shows Paul's and Rob's run on the same axes.

   b. What is the total time each runner took to run the race? Which runner finished first?

CME Project • *Algebra 1 Teaching Resources*

Additional Practice

1. Messenger Service A charges $15 for pick up and $1.50 per mile for delivery. Messenger Service B charges $9 for pick up and $2.00 per mile for delivery.
   a. If the delivery distance is 10 miles, which company charges less? How much less?
   b. If the delivery distance is 25 miles, which company charges less? How much less?
   c. At what point will both companies charge the same amount?

2. Use substitution to find the intersection point of the graphs of the system of equations.
   a. $y = 6 - 2x$ and $4x + 2y = 8$
   b. Graph each equation. What do the graphs suggest about the solution to the system of equations?

3. What is the solution to each system of equations? If there is no solution, explain.
   a. $y = 19x + 92$ and $y = 25x - 40$
   b. $y = 23x + 175$ and $y = 23x - 150$

4. Identify the graphs of each pair of equations as *parallel, intersecting,* or *identical.* Explain.

   a. $y = \frac{2}{5}x + 7$ and $y = 0.4x - 1$ b. $3x - 2y = 1$ and $2x - 3y = -1$

   c. $3x + 2y = 5$ and $-3x - 2y = -5$ d. $2x - 3y = 6$ and $y = \frac{2}{3}x - 6$

5. Write an equation of the line that contains the given point and is parallel to the given line.

   a. $(12, -3); y = -\frac{5}{6}x - 3$ b. $(-6, -5); 2x - 3y = 12$

   c. $(1, -4); y - 2 = -\frac{2}{3}(x + 11)$ d. $(-2, -11); x = -12\frac{2}{5}$

   e. $(-2, -11); y = 15.75$

6. What is the value of k such that the graph of the equation will pass through $(0, -8)$?
   a. $y = 5x + k$ b. $y = 6x + k$ c. $y = 7x + k$
   d. $y = 100x + k$ e. $y = qx + k$
   f. What pattern do you notice about the values of k?

7. What is the value of k such that the graph of the equation will pass through $(-8, 0)$?
   a. $y = 5x + k$ b. $y = 6x + k$ c. $y = 7x + k$
   d. $y = 100x + k$ e. $y = qx + k$
   f. What is the relationship between k and the slope?

Additional Practice

1. Use elimination to solve each system of equations. Check that your solution satisfies both equations.

   a. $x + y = 3$
      $x - y = 7$

   b. $5a - 2b = -7$
      $-5a + 6b = -9$

   c. $5x + 2y = 51$
      $7x - 2y = 9$

   d. $-9x + 3y = -2$
      $9x - 12y = -10$

   e. $3a - 5b = 4$
      $3a + 10b = 10$

   f. $y = 3x - 44$
      $y = -2x + 16$

2. At a wash-and-fold, 2 washing machine loads and 4 dryer loads cost $11.00. Four washing machine loads and 4 dryer loads cost $16.00.

   a. What is the cost of one washing machine load?

   b. What is the cost of one dryer load?

3. **a.** What is the intersection point P of the graphs of $3x + 4y = 18$ and $7x - 3y = -32$?

   b. Write the equation of the vertical line that contains point P.

   c. Write the equation of the horizontal line that contains point P.

   d. Write the equation that results when you subtract the second equation in part (a) from the first equation in part (a). Show that point P satisfies the resulting equation.

4. Write the equations of two lines with slopes -3 and $\frac{3}{4}$ that intersect at the point $(-5, 8)$.

5. Write the equation of a line that does not intersect with the line $3x - 5y = 25$.

6. At a bagel shop, 2 coffees and 4 bagels cost $6.00. Two coffees and 7 bagels cost $8.25.

   a. What is the price of 3 bagels?

   b. What is the price of 1 bagel?

   c. What is the price of 2 coffees?

   d. What is the price of 1 coffee?

   e. What combination of coffees and bagels, if any, would cost $9.00?

7. What is the point of intersection of each pair of graphs? Check that this point satisfies both equations.

   a. $y = 4x - 7$
      $3x - 5y = -33$

   b. $b = -5a + 8$
      $b = 11a + 104$

   c. $5p - 7q = -1$
      $-3p - 7q = 23$

   d. $3m - 5n = 36$
      $-4m - 5n = 22$

   e. $18x - 2y = 8$
      $-3x + 5y = 22$

   f. $7v - 6w = 60$
      $-6v + 8w = -60$

8. Solve each system.

   a. $5x + 3y = 8$
      $4x - 2y = -20$

   b. $10x + 3y = 7$
      $2x - 9y = -5$

   c. $3x - 4y = 10$
      $9x - 12y = -10$

Additional Practice

1. Use algebra and a graphing calculator. Solve each inequality.

   a. $2x + 7 < -3x + 18$ **b.** $|x + 3| > 5$

   c. $4(x - 1)^2 < 324$ **d.** $(x + 2)^2 \geq 0.04$

   e. $(x - 3)^2 \leq -0.9$ **f.** $-x^2 < -|x|$

2. **a.** Use algebra and testing intervals. Solve the inequality
     $15.7x + 22.6 \leq -12.1x - 12.15$.

   b. Use a graphing calculator. Plot $y = 15.7x + 22.6$ and $y = -12.1x - 12.15$
     on the same axes. Is it more difficult or less difficult to use a graphing
     calculator to solve this exercise? Explain.

3. Use a graphing calculator. Graph $y = \frac{x + 9}{2}$ and $y = \sqrt{9x}$ on the same axes.
   Use the graphs to solve the inequality $\frac{x + 9}{2} < \sqrt{9x}$.

4. Explain how you can use this graph to draw a number line for the
   solutions to $x^2 + 5x + 4 \leq 0$. Then draw the number line.

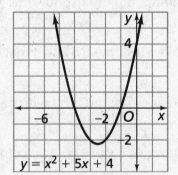

5. **a.** Sketch the graphs of $y = x^2$ and $y = \sqrt{x}$ on the same axes.

   b. Find all the values of x such that $x^2 > \sqrt{x}$.

   c. Draw your solution set on a number line.

6. **a.** Draw a number line to represent $x \leq -5$.

   b. Draw a number line to represent $x > -11$.

   c. How can the number lines from parts (a) and (b) be combined to show
     a number line for $-11 < x \leq -5$?

   d. What x-values make $x \leq -5$, $x > -11$, or both true? How does that look
     on a number line?

7. For each inequality, graph the solution on a number line.

   a. $x \geq -2$ **b.** $(x + 3) \geq -2$

   c. $(x - 7) \geq -2$ **d.** $3x - 4 < 5$

   e. $3(x - 1) - 4 < 5$ **f.** $3(x + 4) - 4 < 5$

Additional Practice

1. **Multiple Choice** Which equation best represents the data in the graph?

   A. $y = -2x + 3$

   B. $y = \frac{3}{5}x - 3$

   C. $y = -\frac{3}{5}x - 3$

   D. $y = -\frac{3}{5}x + 3$

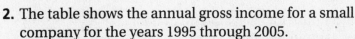

2. The table shows the annual gross income for a small company for the years 1995 through 2005.
   a. How can you use the table to determine if all the points are on a line?
   b. Plot the data points. Is there a linear trend?
   c. Find and plot the balance point. Is the balance point along the trend?

Year	Income (thousands)
1995	$518
1996	$520
1997	$535
1998	$560
1999	$550
2000	$572
2001	$575
2002	$568
2003	$582
2004	$591
2005	$589

3. Plot each data set. Is there a linear trend to the data?

   a.
   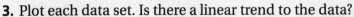

x	y
1	7
2	6
3	5
4	3
5	1

   b.

x	y
1	7
2	3
3	0
4	2
5	6

   c.

x	y
1	3.5
3	3.8
5	4.1
7	3.9
9	4.2

4. For each table in Exercise 3, calculate the balance point $(\bar{x}, \bar{y})$. Plot it along with the data.

5. For each table with a linear trend in Exercise 3, estimate the slope of the trend. Use the balance point you found in Exercise 4 to write a trend line equation. Graph each trend line on the same plot as your data.

6. These data at the right follow a linear trend.
   a. Plot the points.
   b. **Multiple Choice** Graph each line on the same axes. Which line do you think fits the data best?

   A. $y = -x + 10$ **B.** $y = -2x + 20$ **C.** $y = -1.5x + 15$

x	y
3	11.1
4	8.7
5	7.8
6	5.2
7	4.2
8	2.9

Additional Practice

Convert days to weeks. Round your answer to the nearest tenth of a week.

1. 112 days   **2.** 214 days   **3.** 331 days   **4.** 365 days

Convert yards to feet.

5. 19 yards   **6.** 350 yards   **7.** 1760 yards   **8.** 10,000 yards

For Exercises 9–11, a building company estimates that the cost of building a house is $55 for each square foot of floor space.

9. Calculate the cost of building a house for each amount of floor space.
   a. 1800 square feet   **b.** 2500 square feet   **c.** 5250 square feet

10. The amount of floor space in a house is h square feet. Find a rule to calculate the building company's estimated cost.

11. What is the building company's estimated cost to build a rectangular room with dimensions 22 feet by 27 feet?

12. Decide whether each description represents a function. Explain.
   a. The input is a page number of this workbook. The output is the number of words on that page.
   b. The input is the area of a square. The output is the perimeter of that square.
   c. The input is the area of a rectangle. The output is the perimeter of that rectangle.

13. A city sign shows the current time and current temperature. Can you refer to time and temperature as the variables in a function? If so, which is the independent variable and which is the dependent variable? Explain.

14. Use a calculator's square root button. Find the square root of 0.06. Find the square root of the result. Then find the square root of that result. Continue this pattern at least 35 times. What is your final output?

15. Explain your results when you follow the steps in Exercise 14 with any number between 0.01 and 0.05.

16. Use a calculator's $\boxed{+/-}$ key to represent the function $x \mapsto -x$.
   a. Let $x = 0.06$ and apply the rule. Describe your result. Use the output as the next input, and apply the rule again. Repeat the process at least five times. Explain your results.
   b. Choose a value of x between 0.01 and 0.05. Repeat the process in part (a).
   c. How are the outputs in parts (a) and (b) similar? How are the outputs different?

Additional Practice

For Exercises 1–5, use these four functions.

$$g(t) = 10 + 4t \qquad h(t) = t^2 - 4 \qquad t \overset{j}{\mapsto} 5(t + 5) \qquad t \overset{k}{\mapsto} 5t - 4$$

1. For which function(s) is the output 21 for an input of 5?

2. Which function results in this input-output table?

3. What input(s), if any, give the same outputs for function g and for function k?

Input	Output
0	25
1	30

4. What input(s), if any, give the same outputs for function g and for function j?

5. What input(s), if any, give the same outputs for function j and for function k?

This number trick always results in the same number. Pick a number. Add 1. Square the result. Subtract 1. Divide by the original number. Finally, subtract the original number.

6. Choose at least three different numbers as inputs for the number trick function. Write the input-output pairs in a table.

7. Use the input x as the starting number. Apply each step of the number trick and record the result of each step. What is the final result?

For Exercises 8–11, use the functions $p(x) = x^2 + 8$ and $q(x) = |5 - 2x|$. Evaluate each function.

8. $p(0)$, $p(2)$, and $p(-2)$

9. $q(0)$, $q(3)$, and $q(-3)$

10. $p(5) - 8$

11. $p(-5) + q(-5)$

12. Let d represent a function that uses two points as inputs and gives back a number as an output. The two input points are $P(x_1, y_1)$ and $Q(x_2, y_2)$.

$$d(P, Q) = \sqrt{(x_1 - x_2)^2 + (y_1 - y_2)^2}$$

Calculate $d(P, Q)$ when P is (3, 10) and Q is (15, 5).

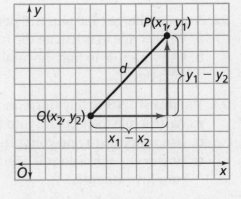

For Exercises 13–20, use the functions $r(x) = 5x - 3$ and $s(x) = \frac{x + 3}{5}$ to evaluate each function.

13. $r(1)$

14. $r(r(1))$

15. $r(r(r(1)))$

16. $s(7)$

17. $s(s(7))$

18. $r(s(12))$

19. $s(r(12))$

20. $r(r(s(s(7))))$

Name _____ Class _____ Date _____

Additional Practice

Determine the domain for each function.

1. $f(x) = x + 3$

2. $x \mapsto (x + 3)^2$

3. $g(x) = \dfrac{1}{x + 3}$

4. $x \mapsto \sqrt{x + 3}$

5. $h(x) = x^2 + 3$

6. $x \mapsto |x + 3|$

Use the functions $f(x) = 2x + 3$, $g(x) = \dfrac{x + 6}{2}$, **and** $h(x) = \dfrac{3}{x + 2}$ **to find each of the following.**

7. $f(4)$

8. $g(4)$

9. $h(4)$

10. $f(g(4))$

11. $f(h(4))$

12. $h(f(x))$

Decide whether each graph is the graph of a function. Explain.

13.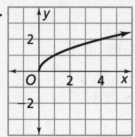

14.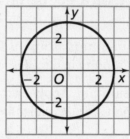

15.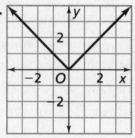

For Exercises 16–21, graph each function.

16. $f(x) = 4x + 2$

17. $f(x) = -\dfrac{2}{3}x + 6$

18. $f(x) = |x| - 1$

19. $x \mapsto -|x + 2|$

20. $x \mapsto 2x^2$

21. $x \mapsto -x^2$

22. A resort charges $50 plus $10 per person to rent a cabin for a day.
   a. Write a rule to calculate the total cost of renting a cabin for a day.
   b. Use your rule to find the total cost for six people to stay in a cabin for a day.

23. You invest $209 to buy shirts and sell them for $9.50 each.
   a. Write a rule to calculate your profit.
   b. Use your rule to find your profit after selling 24 shirts.
   c. How many shirts do you need to sell in order to make back your investment?

Additional Practice

A company is drilling for oil. The table shows how the volume of earth removed from the hole increases as the hole gets deeper.

Depth of Hole (feet)	Volume of Earth (cubic feet)
100	1257
200	2514
300	3771
400	5028
500	6285

1. What volume of earth does the oil company remove when the hole is 700 feet deep? 1200 feet deep? Explain.

2. Write an equation describing the relationship between depth D and volume V.

3. Use your equation from Exercise 2. Determine the depth of the hole when the oil company removes 5153.7 cubic feet of earth.

For Exercises 4 and 5, use Tables A, B, and C.

Table A

Input	Output	Δ
−1		−1
0		−1
1		−1
2	−5	−1
3	−6	

Table B

Input	Output	Δ
0	3	
1	4	
2	7	
3	12	
4	19	

Table C

Input	Output	Δ
0		5
2	5	5
4		5
6		5
8		

4. List the information that is missing from each table.

5. Which tables can you generate using a linear function? Write each linear function.

6. **Multiple Choice** The table shows the monthly cost of a cell phone plan based on the number of minutes used. What is the monthly cost for 20 minutes of calls?
   A. $30.20 **B.** $33.00 **C.** $33.15 **D.** $50.00

Minutes Used	Monthly Cost
1	$30.15
2	$30.30
3	$30.45

For Exercises 7–10, graph the data for each table. For each table that matches a linear function, write that function.

7.
Input	Output
0	5
1	7
2	13
3	23
4	41

8.
Input	Output
0	$\frac{1}{4}$
1	1
2	$1\frac{3}{4}$
3	$2\frac{1}{2}$
4	$3\frac{1}{4}$

9.
Input	Output
0	6
1	3
2	0
3	−3
4	−6

10.
Input	Output
0	24
1	8
2	$2\frac{2}{3}$
3	$\frac{8}{9}$
4	$\frac{8}{27}$

Additional Practice

For Exercises 1 and 2, make a table for each recursive rule. Use inputs 0, 1, 2, and 3. Then decide whether Rule 1 and Rule 2 define the same function.

1. Rule 1: $x \mapsto 2^x$
Rule 2: The first input-output pair is (0, 1). To find other outputs, start with the first output and add 1, then add 2, then add 3, and so on.

2. Rule 1: $x \mapsto 2 - x$
Rule 2: The first input-output pair is (0, 2). To find each output after the first, take the previous output and subtract 1.

3. A new car costs $30,000. At the end of each year, the car is worth 85% of its start-of-year value. Write a recursive rule that describes the value of the car. What is the value of the car at the end of 5 years?

Last month, a worker marked the water level in a cylindrical tank. During the month, the water level went down 50 feet below the worker's mark. Assume the worker's mark is "zero." Today the worker fills the tank. The water level increases by 8 feet per hour.

4. Calculate the height of the water today for each hour from 0 to 8 hours. Make a table showing your results.

5. Describe the pattern in the output values. Can a linear function generate this table? If so, write the function.

6. How many hours will it take for the water level in the tank to reach a height of 75 feet above the worker's zero mark? Round your answer to a whole number. Explain.

For Exercises 7 and 8, use the pattern. Stage 1 has a row with 1 dot. Stage 2 adds a row of 2 dots, Stage 3 adds a row of 3 dots, Stage 4 adds a row of 4 dots, and so on.

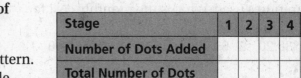

Stage 1 | Stage 2 | Stage 3 | Stage 4

Stage	1	2	3	4	5	6
Number of Dots Added						
Total Number of Dots						

7. Draw Stages 5 and 6 of this pattern. Use them to complete the table.

8. Write a recursive rule that describes the pattern in the total number of dots.

For Exercises 9–10, make a table for each recursive rule. Use the integers 0 to 5 for input values. If possible, find a linear function that generates each table.

	Inputs	Output
9. Rule A	$\begin{cases} 0 \\ 1 \text{ to } 5 \end{cases}$	5 3 times the previous output
10. Rule B	$\begin{cases} 0 \\ 1 \text{ to } 5 \end{cases}$	4 3 less than the previous output

Additional Practice

In Exercises 1–3, Monica is at a bowling center. By becoming a member for $30, she gets a 15% discount on her bowling cost.

1. Build a function-machine network using the nonmember bowling cost as the input. The output is Monica's bowling cost with membership.

2. Suppose b is the cost of one night's bowling for nonmembers. Find a rule for $M(b)$, Monica's discounted cost. Do not include the membership fee.

3. For what values of b does Monica save money by becoming a member? Explain.

At the bowling center, bowlers pay $3 per game for duckpin bowling and $5 per game for candlepin bowling. On Saturday night, bowlers play a total of 180 games.

4. At the end of the night, a clerk estimates that twice as many people bowled duckpins as bowled candlepins. Based on that estimate, what was the total amount of money spent for the 180 games? Explain.

5. The cashier reports that the actual total for the 180 games is $680. How many games of each type did bowlers play?

During one month, a computer programmer works 175 hours and earns $30 per hour.

6. She pays 30% of her total earnings in taxes and puts away 25% of her total earnings for rent. What are the amounts that she pays in taxes and in rent?

7. Of the amount remaining, she saves 15% and puts away $500 for emergencies. She divides the rest into four equal amounts for entertainment, food, clothing, and further education. What amount does she set aside for each of the six categories? Write each amount to the nearest ten dollars.

8. During the previous month, she worked 200 hours at the same hourly rate. Use the information provided in Exercises 7 and 8 to calculate the amounts she set aside for entertainment, food, clothing, and further education. Explain.

In Exercises 9–10, find each set of numbers.

9. The average of two numbers is 19. The difference between them is 8. Find the two numbers.

10. Each of four numbers in a list is six more than the number that precedes it in the list. The sum of the four numbers is 64. Find the four numbers.

Name _____ Class _____ Date _____

Additional Practice

Lesson 5.12

A tank holds 40,000 gallons of water. Twice a day, consumers use one eighth of the amount of water that was in the tank at the beginning of that day.

1. Make an input-output table. Calculate the number of gallons of water that remain in the tank at the end of each day from Day 0 to Day 8. Record the amounts to the nearest gallon.

2. Describe a recursive rule for the situation, using words.

3. Write the recursive rule $W(n)$, the number of gallons of water in the tank after n days.

4. Is this function linear? Is it exponential? Write the rule in closed form.

5. Assuming the pattern continues, when will the amount of water in the tank be less than 1 gallon?

For Exercises 6 and 7, use recursive rules 1 and 2.

Rule 1:
$$r(n) = \begin{cases} 10, & \text{if } n = 1 \\ 5, & \text{if } n = 2 \\ r(n-1) - r(n-2), & \text{if } n > 2 \end{cases}$$

Rule 2:
The first two outputs are 10 and 5. To find each subsequent output, take the previous output and subtract the output before it.

6. Find the first 10 outputs for Rules 1 and 2.

7. Explain why the two rules represent the same function.

8. Explain how to find the 155th output for the function $T(x)$.
$$T(x) = \begin{cases} -5, & \text{if } x = 1 \\ 4, & \text{if } x = 2 \\ T(x-1) - T(x-2), & \text{if } x > 2 \end{cases}$$

9. Use the function definition $G(y) = \begin{cases} N, & \text{if } y = 0 \\ 2[G(y-1)]^2 + N, & \text{if } y > 0 \end{cases}$.

  a. Describe the function using sentences.

  b. What is the output in the long run when you start with $N = 2$? With $N = 0$? With $N = -1$?

For Exercises 10–13, find a closed-form function that gives the same outputs as each recursively defined function.

10. $f(n) = \begin{cases} -5, & \text{if } n = 0 \\ f(n-1) + 2, & \text{if } n > 0 \end{cases}$

11. $h(n) = \begin{cases} -7, & \text{if } n = 0 \\ h(n-1) - 1, & \text{if } n > 0 \end{cases}$

12. $g(n) = \begin{cases} 8, & \text{if } n = 0 \\ g(n-1) - 3, & \text{if } n > 0 \end{cases}$

13. $k(n) = \begin{cases} -q, & \text{if } n = 0 \\ k(n-1) + p, & \text{if } n > 0 \end{cases}$

Name _____ Class _____ Date _____

Additional Practice

1. Rewrite each expression using exponents.

   a. $x \cdot x \cdot y \cdot x \cdot x \cdot y$ **b.** $a \cdot 3 \cdot b^2 \cdot a^2 \cdot 3 \cdot b$ **c.** $m \cdot m^6 \cdot m \cdot 3m$

   d. $(2a)^2 \cdot (2a)^2 \cdot (2a) \cdot a^3$ **e.** $(3x)^2 \cdot (2x)^3$ **f.** $2 \cdot 3 \cdot 4 \cdot x \cdot x^2 \cdot x^3$

2. What is the value of s in each equation?

   a. $3^s = 81$ **b.** $3^{s-2} = 81$ **c.** $3^{2s} = 81$

   d. $3^s \cdot 3^s = 729$ **e.** $4^{s-1} = 64$ **f.** $5^s \cdot 5^s \cdot 5^s = 125$

3. Suppose a photocopier makes copies at 125% of the original size.
   A picture is 4 inches wide. If each copy serves as the original for the next
   copy, how wide is the picture on each copy?

   a. the first copy   **b.** the second copy

   c. the sixth copy   **d.** the nth copy

4. Suppose a photocopier makes copies at 80% of the original size. Each
   copy serves as the original for the next copy. If the picture is 6 inches
   wide, how wide is the picture on each copy?

   a. the first copy   **b.** the second copy

   c. the sixth copy   **d.** the nth copy

5. Which of the following are identities?

   a. $\left(-\frac{1}{x}\right)^1 = -\left(\frac{1}{x}\right)^1$ **b.** $\left(-\frac{1}{x}\right)^2 = -\left(\frac{1}{x}\right)^2$ **c.** $\left(-\frac{1}{x}\right)^3 = -\left(\frac{1}{x}\right)^3$

   d. $\left(-\frac{1}{x}\right)^4 = -\left(\frac{1}{x}\right)^4$ **e.** $\left(-\frac{1}{x}\right)^5 = -\left(\frac{1}{x}\right)^5$ **f.** What is the pattern?

6. Decide whether each expression equals 7^8, without using a calculator.
   Explain each result.

   a. $7 \cdot 7 \cdot 7 \cdot 7 \cdot 7 \cdot 7 \cdot 7$ **b.** $7^4 \cdot 7^2$ **c.** $\frac{7^{16}}{7^2}$ **d.** $\frac{7^4 \cdot 7^3 \cdot 7^3}{7^2}$

7. Write each expression as a single power of m.

   a. $(m^3)^5$ **b.** $(m^5)^3$ **c.** $(m^9)^9$ **d.** $\frac{m^{15}}{m^{12}}$ **e.** $\frac{1}{m^4}(m^9)$

8. For each sequence, find a pattern. Use your pattern to write the next three
   terms in each sequence.

   a. 729, 243, 81   **b.** 10,000; 1000; 100   **c.** $8^3, 8^2, 8^1$

   d. $\frac{1}{625}, \frac{1}{125}, \frac{1}{25}$ **e.** $\left(\frac{1}{3}\right)^3, \left(\frac{1}{3}\right)^2, \left(\frac{1}{3}\right)^1$ **f.** $5^5, 5^4, 5^3$

Additional Practice

1. Simplify each expression. Assume that $x \neq 0$ and $y \neq 0$.

   a. $(2x + 15y)^0$
   b. $5 \cdot (4x^2y - 2xy^2)^0$
   c. $x^0 + y^0 + (x + y)^0$

2. Decide whether each expression equals 4^{-8}, without using a calculator. Explain each result.

   a. $(4^{-4}) \cdot 4^2$
   b. $4^{-6} \cdot 4^{-2}$
   c. $(4^{-5})^{-3}$

   d. $(4^2)^{-4}$
   e. $\dfrac{4^5}{4^{13}}$
   f. $\left(\dfrac{1}{4}\right)^8$

   g. $\dfrac{1}{4^{-8}}$
   h. $\left(\dfrac{1}{4^4}\right)^{-2}$

3. Write each expression as a single power of p.

   a. $(p^{-6})(p^{11})$
   b. $((p^2)^3)^{-5}$

   c. $\dfrac{(p^0)^4}{p^6}$
   d. $\dfrac{(p^5)^0}{(p^0)(p^{-2})}$

4. Find each sum.

   a. 3^0
   b. $3^0 + 3^1$

   c. $3^0 + 3^1 + 3^2$
   d. $3^0 + 3^1 + 3^2 + 3^3$

   e. $3^0 + 3^1 + 3^2 + 3^3 + 3^4$
   f. What is the pattern of the results?

5. Write each number in scientific notation.

   a. 1,000,000
   b. 47,500
   c. 512,000,000

   d. 202,000
   e. 0.00231
   f. 0.00003579

   g. $(4.1 \times 10^5)(4 \times 10^7)$
   h. $(12 \times 10^3)(9 \times 10^4)$
   i. $153,000 + 2,017,000$

6. Write each number in decimal notation.

   a. 2.53×10^5
   b. 4.1032×10^{11}
   c. 1.59×10^{-5}

   d. 4.72×10^{-8}
   e. 7.2×10^0
   f. 5.06×10^{12}

7. Find the mean and median of each set of numbers.

   a. $1.2 \times 10^3, 3.4 \times 10^4, 1.6 \times 10^2, 9.8 \times 10^3, 7.5 \times 10^4$
   b. $3.21 \times 10^4, 14.5 \times 10^2, 28.2 \times 10^3, 115 \times 10^0, 228 \times 10^3$

8. Express each product or quotient in scientific notation.

   a. $(5 \times 10^7)^3$
   b. $(4 \times 10^9)^2$
   c. $(6.2 \times 10^5)^2$

   d. $\dfrac{6 \times 10^{12}}{3 \times 10^5}$
   e. $\dfrac{9.3 \times 10^{11}}{3 \times 10^5}$
   f. $\dfrac{5.2 \times 10^{10}}{4 \times 10^7}$

Additional Practice

1. Find all of the prime numbers with square roots between 4 and 5.

2. Write each expression as the square root of an integer. Let $m = \sqrt{5}$, $n = \sqrt{6}$, and $p = \sqrt{11}$.
   a. mn b. mp c. np
   d. Does $m + n = p$?
   e. What is the product of your results for parts (a), (b), and (c)?

3. Find the value of each expression. Let $x = \dfrac{1}{\sqrt{3}}$, $y = \dfrac{1}{3}$, and $z = \dfrac{\sqrt{8}}{3}$.
   a. $3x^2$ b. $y^2 + z^2$

4. The formula for the surface area of a cube is $A = 6s^2$, where s is the length of a side of the cube. Find the length of the side of each cube with the given surface area.
   a. 6 cm^2 b. 24 cm^2 c. 12 cm^2 d. 18 cm^2

5. Determine whether each square root is an integer. For each square root that is not an integer, find the two integers it lies between.
   a. $\sqrt{12}$ b. $\sqrt{15}$ c. $\sqrt{16}$ d. $\sqrt{21}$ e. $\sqrt{26}$
   f. What is the least positive integer with a square root that is greater than 6?

6. Notice that you can simplify $\sqrt{45}$ by rewriting it as $\sqrt{9} \cdot \sqrt{5} = 3\sqrt{5}$. Using a similar method, simplify each expression.
   a. $\sqrt{24}$ b. $\sqrt{500}$ c. $\sqrt{3^5 \cdot 7^3}$

7. For each equation, find the integer p that satisfies the equation.
   a. $\sqrt{32} - \sqrt{2} = p\sqrt{2}$ b. $\sqrt{75} + \sqrt{3} = p\sqrt{3}$
   c. $\sqrt{125} - 4\sqrt{5} = p\sqrt{5}$ d. $\sqrt{44} + 3\sqrt{11} = p\sqrt{11}$

8. Order the following expressions in order from least to greatest.
$$\sqrt{15}, \sqrt{3 \cdot 4}, \frac{\sqrt{15}}{\sqrt{5}}, \sqrt{15 \cdot 5}, \sqrt{15} + \sqrt{5}$$

9. In the diagram, there are four circles that share the same center. The areas of the circles are 4π, 6π, 8π, and 10π. Find a, b, c, and $a + b + c$.

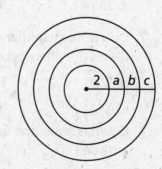

Additional Practice

1. Write each radical in simplified form.

   a. $\sqrt{300}$ **b.** $\sqrt{32}$ **c.** $\sqrt{50}$ **d.** $\sqrt{54}$

   e. $\sqrt{60}$ **f.** $\sqrt{192}$ **g.** $\sqrt{42}$ **h.** $\sqrt{169}$

2. For each right triangle, find the length of the third side. Write your result in simplified form.

   a. legs of 8 in. and 10 in.   **b.** legs of $\frac{1}{3}$ in. and $\frac{1}{4}$ in.

   c. a leg of $\frac{1}{2}$ in. and a hypotenuse of $\frac{3}{4}$ in.

3. Calculate the area and perimeter of each rectangle given its side lengths.

   a. $4\sqrt{6}$ cm and $5\sqrt{6}$ cm   **b.** $6\sqrt{3}$ cm and $2\sqrt{7}$ cm

   c. $\frac{\sqrt{10}}{2}$ cm and $4\sqrt{10}$ cm

4. Here is an input-output table of the function $g(x) = x^5$. Simplify each square root.

   a. $\sqrt{32}$ **b.** $\sqrt{243}$ **c.** $\sqrt{1024}$

   d. $\sqrt{3125}$ **e.** $\sqrt{7776}$ **f.** What is the pattern?

x	x^5
0	0
1	1
2	32
3	243
4	1024
5	3125
6	7776

5. **a.** Show that $\sqrt{13}$ is a real number by locating it on the number line. (*Hint:* Construct a right triangle with a hypotenuse that is a segment of length $\sqrt{13}$.)

   b. Show that $\sqrt{7}$ is a real number by locating it on the number line. (*Hint:* Construct a right triangle with a base that is a segment of length $\sqrt{7}$.)

6. Draw a diagram like the diagram of the sets of $\mathbb{Z}$, $\mathbb{Q}$, and $\mathbb{R}$ in this lesson. Then place each number in the diagram.

   a. $\sqrt{5} - 3$ **b.** $\sqrt{21}$ **c.** $\frac{165}{11}$ **d.** $\frac{121}{9}$

   e. 15.002   **f.** $\sqrt{16} + \sqrt{25}$ **g.** $\sqrt{15} + \sqrt{9}$ **h.** $\sqrt{4.01^2}$

7. Determine whether each square root is an integer. For each square root that is not an integer, find the two integers it lies between.

   a. $\sqrt{21}$ **b.** $\sqrt{22}$ **c.** $\sqrt{28}$ **d.** $\sqrt{30}$

   e. $\sqrt{34}$ **f.** $\sqrt{35}$ **g.** $\sqrt{37}$ **h.** $\sqrt{50}$

   i. What is the greatest positive integer with a square root that is less than 10?

Additional Practice

1. Use the functions $g(x) = \sqrt{(2x)^2}$ and $h(x) = \sqrt[3]{(2x)^3}$.

   a. Make input-output tables for each function. Use inputs that include at least a few negative values.

   b. Graph each function.

   c. How are the two functions similar? How are they different? Have you seen either function before, possibly in a different form?

2. Use the duck principle to show that each equation is true.

   a. $\sqrt[3]{16} \cdot \sqrt[3]{4} = 4$ **b.** $\sqrt[4]{49} = \sqrt{7}$

   c. $\sqrt[3]{6} \cdot \sqrt[6]{5} = \sqrt[6]{180}$ **d.** $\dfrac{\sqrt[4]{99}}{\sqrt[4]{11}} = \sqrt[4]{9}$

   e. $\dfrac{\sqrt[10]{88}}{\sqrt[5]{2}} = \sqrt[10]{22}$ **f.** $\sqrt[5]{5} \cdot \sqrt[5]{12} \cdot \sqrt[5]{10} \cdot \sqrt[5]{600}$

3. Use the fact that $1{,}048{,}576 = 4^{10}$. Simplify each radical.

   a. $\sqrt{1{,}048{,}576}$ **b.** $\sqrt[3]{1{,}048{,}576}$ **c.** $\sqrt[4]{1{,}048{,}576}$

   d. $\sqrt[5]{1{,}048{,}576}$ **e.** $\sqrt[6]{1{,}048{,}576}$ **f.** $\sqrt[7]{1{,}048{,}576}$

   g. $\sqrt[8]{1{,}048{,}576}$ **h.** $\sqrt[9]{1{,}048{,}576}$ **i.** $\sqrt[10]{1{,}048{,}576}$

   j. Which of the numbers in parts (a)–(i) are integers? Explain.

4. The volume of the larger cube is three times the volume of the smaller cube.

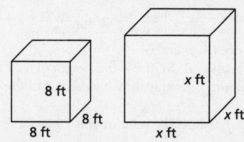

8 ft   8 ft   8 ft   x ft   x ft   x ft

   a. If each side of the smaller cube is 8 ft long, find the volume of each cube.

   b. Show that each side of the larger cube is not three times longer than the side of the smaller cube.

   c. How long is each side of the larger cube?

5. Find the value of p that satisfies each equation.

   a. $\sqrt{6} \cdot \sqrt{p} = 6$ **b.** $\sqrt[3]{6} \cdot \sqrt[3]{p} = 6$ **c.** $\sqrt[4]{6} \cdot \sqrt[4]{p} = 6$

   d. $\sqrt[5]{6} \cdot \sqrt[5]{p} = 6$ **e.** $\sqrt[6]{6} \cdot \sqrt[6]{p} = 6$ **f.** What is the pattern?

Additional Practice

1. Use a calculator and sketch the graph of $y = 800(1.06)^x$ using the domain $0 \leq x \leq 20$. Describe a situation that this graph represents.

2. Rasheed puts $1000 into an investment account at 8% APR compounded annually. After how many years will he be closest to doubling his initial investment? Tripling his investment? Quadrupling his investment?

3. For each interest rate compounded annually, find the number of years after which Rasheed would be closest to tripling his starting investment of $1000.

   a. 5%   **b.** 10%   **c.** 15%   **d.** 20%

4. Suppose you invest $5000. Calculate the total value of each investment after two years.

   a. 3% APR compounded annually   **b.** 3% APR compounded quarterly

   c. 5% APR compounded annually   **d.** 5% APR compounded monthly

5. Jodi invests $5000 for three years. How much will she earn in an account with each interest rate compounded annually?

   a. 4% APR   **b.** 5% APR   **c.** 6% APR

   d. 8% APR   **e.** 10% APR   **f.** 12% APR

6. Ernie drops a ball from a height of 64 feet. On its first bounce, the ball rebounds to 48 feet. On its second bounce, it rebounds to 36 feet. On its third bounce, it rebounds to 27 feet.

   a. Show that the ratios $\dfrac{\text{bounce 1}}{\text{starting height}}$, $\dfrac{\text{bounce 2}}{\text{bounce 3}}$, and $\dfrac{\text{bounce 3}}{\text{bounce 2}}$ are equal.

   b. Find the heights of bounces 4, 5, and 6.

   c. Use your data from parts (a) and (b). If h is the height of a certain bounce, write an expression that represents the height of the next bounce in terms of h.

   d. Write an equation that represents the relationship between height h and bounce b.

7. Sketch each graph for $-3 \leq x \leq 3$.

   a. $y = 3^x$ **b.** $y = 1^x$ **c.** $y = 5^x$

   d. $y = \left(\dfrac{1}{3}\right)^x$ **e.** $y = 3^{-x}$ **f.** $y = \left(\dfrac{1}{5}\right)^x$

8. Consider the graph of $y = b^{-x}$, where b is any positive real number.

   a. For what values of b is the graph of y increasing?

   b. For what values of b is the graph of y decreasing?

   c. For what values of b is the graph of y neither increasing nor decreasing?

Additional Practice

1. Decide whether you can model each table with a linear function, an exponential function, or neither. Find a linear or exponential function that generates the table, if one exists.

a.
x	y
−2	9
−1	3
0	1
1	$\frac{1}{3}$
2	$\frac{1}{9}$

b.
x	y
−2	−30
−1	−60
1	60
2	30
3	20

c.
x	y
−2	$\frac{1}{4}$
−1	1
0	4
1	16
2	64

d.
x	y
−2	11
−1	8
0	5
1	5
2	−1

2. Find a rule that shows the relationship between x and y in Table A and Table B.

3. Melissa measures her blood glucose level. She records 100 milligrams at noon. After one hour, she records 80 milligrams.
   a. Find a linear equation for the situation. Then find an exponential relationship for the situation.
   b. Use tables to show the linear and exponential relationships. For inputs, use 0 to 5 hours.
   c. Graph each relationship on the same coordinate plane.

Table A
x	y
−3	8
−2	4
−1	2
0	1
1	$\frac{1}{2}$
2	$\frac{1}{4}$
3	$\frac{1}{8}$

Table B
x	y
−3	18
−2	8
−1	2
0	0
1	2
2	8
3	18

For Exercises 4–6, use the functions $f(x) = -x + 6$ and $g(x) = 4x - 3$.

4. Find each value.
   a. $f(0)$ b. $f(5)$ c. $f(-5)$
   d. $g(0)$ e. $g(5)$ f. $g(-5)$

5. Find each value.
   a. $f(g(0))$ b. $g(f(0))$ c. $f(f(0))$ d. $g(g(0))$
   e. $f(g(1))$ f. $g(f(1))$ g. $f(g(-1))$ h. $g(f(-1))$
   i. $f\left(g\left(\frac{1}{4}\right)\right)$ j. $g\left(f\left(\frac{1}{4}\right)\right)$ k. $f\left(g\left(\frac{1}{2}\right)\right)$ l. $g\left(f\left(\frac{1}{2}\right)\right)$

6. Sketch each graph.
   a. f b. g
   c. $h(x) = f(g(x))$ d. $k(x) = g(f(x))$

Additional Practice

1. There are two numbers n that satisfy the following equations. Find both numbers.
   a. $n(n + 1) = 306$
   b. $n(n + 1) = 462$
   c. $(n - 1)(n) = 182$

2. The following function is defined by a messy rule.
   $$p(x) = (x - 2)(x^2 - 2x + 5) - x(x^2 + 4x + 9)$$
   a. What is $p(0)$?
   b. What is $p(5)$?
   c. What is $p(10)$?
   d. Expand the expressions in this function to find a simpler rule for $p(x)$.

3. A square is $(x + 1)$ inches on each side. You cut a smaller square hole from the larger square that is $(y + 1)$ inches on each side. In terms of x and y, find the area of the leftover shape in square inches. Explain your method.

4. Suppose $p(x) = x^4 - 3x^2 + 1$ and $q(x) = (x^2 + x - 1)(x^2 - x - 1)$. Prove that p and q are the same function.

5. Find all of the solutions to each equation.
   a. $(x - 8)(x + 3) = 0$
   b. $(x - 11)(x + 12) = 0$
   c. $3x(x - 6) = 0$
   d. $(x - 2)(x - 3)(x - 4) = 0$

6. What are all the solutions to the equation $x^5 = x^3$?

7. Find all of the solutions to each equation.
   a. $(x + 19)(x + 27) = 0$
   b. $(x + 13)(x + 47) = 0$
   c. $(3x - 4)(x + 1) = 0$
   d. $x(12x + 5) = 0$

8. a. Rewrite $(x + 5)(x + 8)$ in the form $x^2 + (\Box + \Box)x + (\Box \cdot \Box)$.
   b. Suppose $(x + p)(x + q) = x^2 + (4 + 7)x + (4 \cdot 7)$. Use the pattern in part (a) to find p and q.

9. Find an equation with only the solutions listed.
   a. 4 and -7
   b. -4 and 7
   c. -4 and -7
   d. $-4, -7,$ and 0

Additional Practice

1. Find the greatest common factor of each set of expressions.

 a. $10x^4$ and $18x^2$ **b.** $10x^4$ and $40x$

 c. $18p^2$ and $27q^2$ **d.** pq and pr

 e. m^2n and mn^2 **f.** a^3b^3, a^2b^2, and a^2c^3

2. Write each expression as a product of two expressions. One expression should be the greatest common factor of the terms. If there is no common factor, then the answer is the original expression.

 a. $10x^4 - 18x^2$ **b.** $10x^4 + 40x$

 c. $18p^2 - 27q^2$ **d.** $pq + pr$

 e. $m^2n - mn^2$ **f.** $a^3b^3 - a^2b^2 - a^2c^2$

3. Find all solutions to each equation. Use factoring and ZPP.

 a. $10x^3 + 8x^2 = 0$ **b.** $5x = px$

 c. $10x^3 = 25x^2$ **d.** $x^2 = 64x$

 e. $10x^3 - 40x = 0$ **f.** $2x^2 + 2y^2 = 0$

4. Write each expression as a product.

 a. $5x(4x - 1) + 6(4x - 1)$ **b.** $(2x - 3)(3x) + (2x - 3)(5)$

5. Write each expression as a product of expressions.

 a. $4py - 7qy$ **b.** $4px^2 - 7qx^2$

 c. $4p(x - 3) + 7q(x - 3)$ **d.** $4px^2 - 8qx^2$

 e. $4px - 12p + 7qx - 21q$ **f.** $p(r + s) + (r + s)$

6. This graph shows two points on the graph of $y = x^2$.

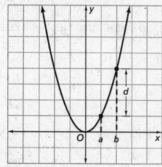

 Show that the vertical distance d is $(b - a)(b + a)$.

7. Expand each expression.

 a. $(x - 1)(x^5 - x^4 - x^3 - x^2 - x - 1)$

 b. $(x - 1)(x^6 - x^5 - x^4 - x^3 - x^2 - x - 1)$

 c. $(x - 1)(x^7 - x^6 - x^5 - x^4 - x^3 - x^2 - x - 1)$

 d. Use the pattern in parts (a)–(c) to find the missing expression in the equation $(x - 1)(\Box) = x^{10} - 2x^9 + 1$.

Additional Practice

1. a. Find two polynomials with the same degree that have a sum of $x^2 + 5x - 3$.
  b. Find two polynomials with different degrees that have a sum of $x^2 + 5x - 3$.
  c. Find two polynomials that have a sum of -10.
  d. Find two polynomials that have a product of $x^2 - 16$.

2. Use $h(x) = x^2 - 3x + 8$.
  a. Find a polynomial $k(x)$ such that $h(x) + k(x) = 3x^2 + 5x + 10$.
  b. Find a polynomial $m(x)$ such that $h(x) + m(x) = 2x^2 - 3$.
  c. Find a polynomial $n(x)$ such that $h(x) + n(x)$ has degree 2 and $h(x)n(x)$ has degree 3.

3. Find the value of d such that $(x + d)(x + 5) = x^2 + 8x + 15$ is an identity.

4. Expand and combine like terms.
  a. $(x - 1)^2 - x^2$
  b. $(x - 1)^3 - x^3$
  c. $(x - 1)^4 - x^4$
  d. $(x - y)^2 - y^2$
  e. $(x - y)^3 - y^3$
  f. $(x - y)^4 - y^4$
  g. $x(x + 1) - x$
  h. $x(x - 1)(x - 2) + x(x - 1)(3)$
  i. $x(x - 1)(x - 2) + x(x - 2)(3)$

5. Transform the expression below into normal form. For what values of b is the coefficient of x equal to zero?
$$(x^2 + 2x + b)(x^2 + 2x - 5)$$

6. Prove that each identity is true. Use basic and derived rules.
  a. $x^{10} - 4 = (x^5 + 2)(x^5 - 2)$
  b. $x^3 + 1 = (x + 1)(x^2 - x + 1)$
  c. $(a + 2b)^2 - (a - 2b)^2 = 8ab$
  d. $(n + 1)^3 - n^2(n + 3) = 3n + 1$
  e. $(x^2 + 2x)(x - 2) = (x^2 - 2x)(x + 2)$
  f. $(x^2 + ax)(x - a) = (x^2 - ax)(x + a)$

7. Show that each equation is an identity.
  a. $4a^2 - b^2 = 2a(2a - b) + b(2a - b)$
  b. $(2a + 1)(2a - b) + (b - 1)(2a - b) = (2a + b)(2a - b)$

8. Find the normal form of each polynomial.
  a. $(1 - x - x^2)(1 - x^3)$
  b. $(1 - x - x^2 - x^3)(1 - x^4)$

Additional Practice

1. Without expanding, find the coefficient of x^3 in the normal form of each polynomial.
   a. $(3x^3 + 2x^2 + 5x + 1)(x^2 - 3)$
   b. $(x + 1)^5$
   c. $(x - 1)(x^6 + x^5 + x^4 + x^3 + x^2 + x + 1)$

2. What is the coefficient of xy^4 in $(x + y)^5$?

3. What is the coefficient of x^4y^2 in $(x + y)^6$?

4. Without expanding, find the coefficient of x^4 in the normal form of
   $(x^3 + 3x^2 + 5x + 8)(3x^2 + 4x + 1) + (5x^5 + 3x^4 + x^3 + 2x^2 + x + 7)$.

5. Find the coefficient of the given term in the normal form of the given polynomial.
   a. x^6; $(x + 1)^6$
   b. x^7; $(x + 1)^7$
   c. x^{10}; $(x + 1)^{10}$
   d. x^{101}; $(x + 1)^{101}$

6. Find the coefficient of each given term in the expanded form of
   $(x + y + z)(x^2 + xy + 2y^2 - 3xz + yz + 2z^2)$.
   a. xyz
   b. x^2y
   c. yz^2
   d. xz^2
   e. y^2z
   f. xy^2

7. Expand each product.
   a. $(1 + x)(1 - x + x^2)$
   b. $(1 + x)(1 - x + x^2 - x^3 + x^4)$
   c. $(1 + x)(1 - x + x^2 - x^3 + x^4 - x^5 + x^6)$

8. Find the normal form of each polynomial.
   a. $(x^4 + x^2 + 1)(x + 1)$
   b. $(x^{12} + x^6 + 1)(x^5 + x^4 + x^3 + x^2 + x + 1)$
   c. $(x^{14} + x^7 + 1)(x^6 + x^5 + x^4 + x^3 + x^2 + x + 1)$

Additional Practice

1. a. Which value of p makes the greatest possible product of $(15 + p)$ and $(15 - p)$? Explain.
   b. Consider all pairs of numbers p and q such that $p + q = 30$. Which pair has the greatest possible product?

2. Solve each equation.
   a. $y^2 - 16 = 0$
   b. $(y - 5)^2 - 36 = 0$
   c. $\left(y - \frac{2}{3}\right)^2 - \frac{1}{9} = 0$
   d. $\left(y - \frac{1}{a}\right)^2 - \frac{1}{b^2} = 0$

3. a. Determine whether $z^{10} - 100 = (z^5 + 10)(z^5 - 10)$ is true. Explain.
   b. What is the degree of $z^{10} - 100$?
   c. What is the degree of $z^5 + 10$? Of $z^5 - 10$? What is the degree of their product?

4. Find all the real numbers that make each equation true.
   a. $x^2 - 25 = 0$
   b. $x^2 - 49 = 0$
   c. $x^2 - 5 = 0$
   d. $x^2 + 25 = 0$
   e. $x^2 + 49 = 0$
   f. $x^2 + 5 = 0$
   g. $x^4 - 81 = 0$
   h. $x^4 - 64 = 0$
   i. $x^4 + 4 = 0$

5. Find the largest prime factor of each number.
   a. $19^2 - 16$
   b. $18^2 - 5^2$
   c. $17^2 - 4$
   d. What is the pattern? Explain.

6. Use the ZPP and what you know about factoring. Find all integer solutions.
   a. $x^2 = 11x - 24$
   b. $x^2 + 49 = 14x$
   c. $(x + 6)(x + 4) = -1$
   d. $x^2 = 11x$
   e. $(x + 3)(x + 4) = 6$
   f. $(x - 6)(x - 4) = 8$

7. Determine whether each expression is a perfect square trinomial. Explain.
   a. $x^2 - 42x - 441$
   b. $x^2 - 24x + 144$
   c. $x^2 + 32x + 256$
   d. $x^2 - 42x + 441$
   e. $x^2 + 24x + 48$
   f. $x^2 - 32x - 256$

8. Factor each quadratic expression over $\mathbb{Z}$. If an expression is not factorable, explain why.
   a. $x^2 + 12x + 36$
   b. $x^2 - 400$
   c. $x^2 + 9x + 8$
   d. $x^2 + 12x + 32$
   e. $x^2 + 400$
   f. $x^2 + 9x + 10$
   g. $x^2 + 12x + 11$
   h. $x^2 + 400x + 399$
   i. $x^2 + 9x + 18$

9. Solve each equation. If no solutions exist, explain why.
   a. $x^2 + 12x + 35 = 0$
   b. $x^2 + 12x = -20$
   c. $x^2 + 12x - 35 = 0$
   d. $x^2 + 12x = 20$

Additional Practice

1. What value of k makes each equation an identity?

 a. $x^2 + 6x = (x + k)^2 - 9$

 b. $x^2 + 8x + 4 = (x + k)^2 - 12$

 c. $x^2 + 7x + 12 = (x + k)^2 - 0.25$

 d. $x^2 + 11x + 15.25 = (x + k)^2 - 15$

2. a. What value of m makes $64t^2 + mt + 9$ a perfect square trinomial?

 b. What value of n makes $81t^2 + 90t + n$ a perfect square trinomial?

3. Solve each polynomial equation. Use completing the square or any other method. Check your answers.

 a. $x^2 - 10x - 16 = -25$

 b. $(3x - 5)(x + 2) = -8$

 c. $x^2 + 4x = 7$

 d. $x^2 - 12x = 1$

 e. $x + 1 = \dfrac{8}{x + 3}$

 f. $x + 3 = \dfrac{27}{x - 3}$

4. Solve the polynomial equation $x^2 - 12x - 5 = 8$ by completing the square. Explain your steps.

5. Solve each polynomial equation. Use completing the square or any other method. Check your answers.

 a. $x^2 - 10x = 20$

 b. $x(x + 12) = 140$

 c. $x^2 + 20x + 17 = 206$

 d. $(x + 3)(x - 9) = 150$

6. A square piece of sheet metal is 18 inches by 18 inches. You cut a small square from each of its corners to form an open-top square box with a bottom area of 196 square inches.

 a. Draw the square sheet. Indicate where to make cuts.

 b. What size squares should you cut from the corners? Show your computations.

 c. What is the area of the original square sheet? What is the area of each square that you cut from the piece of sheet metal?

7. Complete the square for each incomplete polynomial.

 a. $x^2 + 12x$ **b.** $x^2 - 12x$ **c.** $x^2 - 9x$

 d. $x^2 + 9x$ **e.** $x^2 + 24x$ **f.** $x^2 + x$

 g. $x^2 + bx$ **h.** $x^2 - bx$ **i.** $x^2 - \dfrac{b}{2}x$

Additional Practice

1. Solve each equation. If there are no real-number solutions, explain why.
   a. $2x^2 - 5x - 3 = 0$
   b. $2x^2 - 5x + 3 = 0$
   c. $4x^2 - 12x + 9 = 0$
   d. $4x^2 + 12x = 9$
   e. $3x^2 + 2x + 10 = 0$
   f. $2x^2 + x - 3 = 0$

2. Find a value of p such that $2x^2 - 8x + p$ has the following solutions.
   a. two real-number solutions
   b. one real-number solution
   c. no real-number solutions

3. Consider the expression $5x^2 - 3x - 7$.
   a. For what values of x is the expression negative?
   b. For what values of x is the expression positive?
   c. For what values of x is the expression zero?

4. For what values of x is each equation true?
   a. $\left(\dfrac{x+2}{3}\right)^2 - \left(\dfrac{x-2}{3}\right)^2 = 5x$
   b. $\left(\dfrac{x+2}{3}\right)^2 + \left(\dfrac{x-2}{3}\right)^2 = 5x$

5. **a.** Find a quadratic equation with roots -2 and 7.
   b. Can you find a second equation with roots -2 and 7? Can you find a third equation?
   c. Find a quadratic equation with roots 2 and -7.
   d. Can you find a second equation with roots 2 and -7? Can you find a third equation?

6. Suppose you can take square roots of negative numbers. Find two numbers with each following sum and product.
   a. sum of 3, product of 5
   b. sum of 6, product of 15
   c. sum of 1, product of 2

7. Solve each quadratic equation. Find the sum and the product of the roots.
   a. $x^2 - 7x + 2 = 0$
   b. $x^2 - 10x + 2 = 0$
   c. $x^2 + 10x + 8 = 0$
   d. $2x^2 - 5x + 2 = 0$
   e. $x^2 + px + t = 0$
   f. $x^2 + 10x + 20 = 0$
   g. How do the sum and product of the roots relate to the coefficients in each equation?

Additional Practice

1. Find a quadratic equation for the given roots.
   - **a.** 12 and 4
   - **b.** -12 and -4
   - **c.** 8 and 41
   - **d.** $3 + \sqrt{5}$ and $3 - \sqrt{5}$
   - **e.** $-4 + (-\sqrt{7})$ and $-4 - (-\sqrt{7})$
   - **f.** $9 + 3\sqrt{2}$ and $9 - 3\sqrt{2}$

2. Suppose r and s are the roots of the quadratic equation $3x^2 + 2x - 8 = 0$. Find the following values.
   - **a.** $r + s$
   - **b.** rs
   - **c.** the average of r and s

3. **a.** Solve the equation $56x^2 - 103x + 45 = 0$.
   - **b.** Factor the polynomial $56x^2 - 103x + 45$ over $\mathbb{Z}$.
   - **c.** Solve the equation $156x^2 - 347x + 92 = 0$.
   - **d.** Factor the polynomial $156x^2 - 347x + 92$ over $\mathbb{Z}$.
   - **e.** Use your results from parts (a)–(d). Explain how to factor a quadratic over $\mathbb{Z}$.

For Exercises 4–7, factor each polynomial.

4. **a.** $16x^2 - 32x - 9$
   b. $25x^2 - 40x + 7$
   c. $25x^2 + 11x - 14$
   d. $25x^2 + 43x - 14$
   e. $16x^2 + 13x - 3$
   f. $16x^4 + 13x^2 - 3$

5. **a.** $16x^2 - 32xy - 9y^2$
   b. $25x^2 - 40xy + 7y^2$
   c. $25x^2 + 11xy - 14y^2$
   d. $25x^2 + 43xy - 14y^2$

6. **a.** $-20x^2 - 72x - 7$
   b. $-20x^2 + 68x + 7$
   c. $49 - 100x^2$
   d. $20x^3 - 68x^2 - 7x$

7. **a.** $8x^2 + 23x - 3$
   b. $8x^2 + 10x - 3$
   c. $8x^2 - 2x - 3$
   d. $8(x + 1)^2 - 2(x + 1) - 3$
   e. $8x^4 + 23x^2 - 3$
   f. $8(x - 2)^4 + 23(x - 2)^2 - 3$
   g. $(2x^2 + 3)^2 = (x - 1)^2$

8. Solve the equation $3x - \frac{6}{x} = -7$ for x.

Additional Practice

1. Find the minimum value of each function.
   a. $m(x) = (x - 5)^2 - 7$
   b. $n(x) = (x - 5)(x - 11)$
   c. $p(x) = x^2 + 11x - 26$

2. Find a quadratic function that has a minimum value of -15.

3. Of all the pairs of real numbers that add to 32, which pair has the greatest product?

4. Of all the pairs of real numbers that add to 175, which pair has the greatest product?

5. Of all the pairs of real numbers that add to 1001, which pair has the greatest product?

6. What is the minimum value of the function $f(x) = 5x(x - 8)$?

7. You have 208 feet of fence to make a rectangular pen.
   a. What are the dimensions of the rectangle with the maximum area?
   b. Suppose one side of the pen will be against a wall, so it requires no fence. What are the dimensions of the rectangle with the maximum area?

For Exercises 8–12, use the function $f(x) = x^2 + 8x + 15$.

8. Find the minimum value of $f(x)$.

9. Find the value of x that gives the minimum. For Exercises 10–12, refer to this number as m.

10. Calculate $f(m + 1)$ and $f(m - 1)$.

11. Calculate $f(m + 2)$ and $f(m - 2)$.

12. What do you notice about your results from Exercises 10 and 11?

Additional Practice

1. For each equation, sketch its graph. Find each vertex and line of symmetry.

   a. $y - 4 = -3(x + 5)^2$ **b.** $y + 5 = \frac{1}{3}(x - 3)^2$ **c.** $y = 2(x + 3)^2 - 7$

   d. $y = -\frac{1}{4}(x - 6)^2 + 5$ **e.** $(x + 2)^2 = y - 4$

2. The graph of a quadratic function passes through the origin and has vertex (4, 16).

   a. Use symmetry to identify one other point that must be on the graph of this function.

   b. Find an equation for this function.

3. In the equation $x = 2y^2$, y is not a function of x.

   a. Find at least seven points on the graph of $x = 2y^2$.

   b. Use your points to sketch the graph of $x = 2y^2$.

4. Two numbers have a sum of 36.

   a. Write an equation for the product of the two numbers.

   b. Use roots to explain why the maximum product must occur when the two numbers are both 18.

   c. Rewrite the equation you wrote in part (a) in vertex form.

5. Consider the quadratic function $y = 3x^2 - 30x + 85$.

   a. Find the vertex of the function's graph.

   b. Write the equation in vertex form.

   c. Find the y-intercept using either form.

6. A quadratic function has zeros -3 and 9. It passes through point (6, 11). What is the vertex of the graph?

7. Find the roots of the quadratic function $y = x^2 + 16x + 60$.

8. The line of symmetry for $y = x^2 + 16x + 60$ is $x = -8$. Find the equations of three different quadratics that also have $x = -8$ as the line of symmetry. Make sure that each equation has a different value of a.

9. A quadratic function in the form $y = x^2 - 10x + c$ has the line of symmetry $x = 5$. The location of the vertex depends on the value of c.

   a. If $c = 0$, where is the vertex?

   b. Find a value of c that makes the vertex (5, 0).

   c. If $c = 47$, where is the vertex?

   d. Find the coordinates of the vertex in terms of c.

10. For parts (a)–(c), find the value of c such that each function has the given vertex.

    a. $y = x^2 - 12x + c$, vertex (6, 0)   **b.** $y = x^2 - 8x + c$, vertex (4, 0)

    c. $y = x^2 + 16x + c$, vertex (−8, 0)   **d.** Find the vertex of $y = (x - 11)^2$.

    e. Find the vertex of $y = x^2 + 22x - 7$.

Additional Practice

1. Find the number of solutions to each equation.
   a. $x^2 = 25$ b. $x^2 = 0$ c. $x^2 = -25$
   d. $4x + 3 = 2x - 7$ e. $17x + 0.5 = 17x - 0.6$ f. $(x - 2)^3 = \sqrt{x}$
   g. $x^2 = 8$ h. $x^3 = 8$ i. $\sqrt{x} = 8$

2. a. Describe the graph of the equation $y = 10$.
   b. Use the graphing method and a graphing calculator to find both solutions to the equation $x^2 - 2x - 5 = 10$.
   c. Find the values of x that make the inequality $x^2 - 2x - 5 < 10$ true.
   d. Find the values of x that make the inequality $x^2 - 2x - 5 > 10$ true.

For Exercises 3–5, use the graphing method to solve each equation.

3. a. $7(x + 3) = 4x + 15$ b. $7x + 21 = 4x + 15$
   c. $7x = 4x - 6$ d. $3x = -6$
   e. $x = -2$

4. a. $x^2 = 9$ b. $x^2 - 9 = 0$

5. a. $7x + x^2 = 60$ b. $x^2 + 7x - 60 = 0$

6. The figure shows the graphs of $y = x^2 + 5x - 3$ and $y = -x + 3$.
   a. According to the graph, how many solutions are there to the following equation?
   $$x^2 + 5x - 3 = -x + 3$$
   b. Use the graphs to find all values of x that make the equation true.

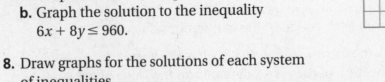

7. a. Graph the line with equation $6x + 8y = 960$.
   b. Graph the solution to the inequality $6x + 8y \leq 960$.

8. Draw graphs for the solutions of each system of inequalities.
   a. $x + y > 5$ and $x - y > 3$ b. $y \leq 6$ and $x \geq 2$
   c. $3x + 4y < 12$ and $2x + 6y > 12$ d. $y \geq x^2$ and $y \leq 2$
   e. $y > |x|$ and $x < 2$

9. a. Describe how the graph of $y < |x|$ compares to the graph of $y = |x|$.
   b. Describe how the graph of $y > x^3 + 7$ compares to the graph of $y = x^3 + 7$.
   c. A graph has shading above the curve that represents the equation $y = f(x)$. Write the inequality that the graph shows.

Additional Practice

1. Is there a quadratic function that fits each table? If so, find the function. If not, explain.

a.

n	y(n)
0	−3
1	−1
2	3
3	9
4	17

b.

n	y(n)
0	4
1	1
2	0
3	1
4	4

c.

n	y(n)
0	1
1	2
2	4
3	8
4	16

2. Does each table match a quadratic function? Explain.

a.

n	y(n)
15	100
16	110
17	128
18	153
19	188

b.

n	y(n)
11	541.5
12	627.5
13	719.5
14	817.5
15	921.5

3. Find a function that agrees with each table.

a.

n	b(n)
0	6
1	8
2	20
3	42
4	74

b.

n	c(n)
0	−10
1	−1
2	4
3	5
4	2

4. Show that the table at the right does not match a linear, quadratic, or cubic function.

5. Make an input-output table for each function. Use the inputs 0 through 5.
  a. $f(x) = (x − 2)(x − 7)$
  b. $g(x) = (x − 4)(x − 2)$
  c. $h(x) = x(x + 7)$
  d. $j(x) = 2(x + 3)(x − 1)$
  e. any function $k(x)$ in which $k(1)$ and $k(2)$ both equal 0

Input	Output
0	3
1	19
2	39
3	70
4	121
5	200

Practice Workbook Answers

Chapter 1

Lessons 1.2 and 1.3
Additional Practice

1. 9
2. −9

3. 11
4. −16

5. If you subtract 11 from the starting number, you will get the ending number.

6. 38
7. 28

8. 18
9. 8

10. −2
11. −12

12. −22
13. −32

14. If the difference is positive, the last digit is 8. If the difference is negative, the last digit is 2.

15. true
16. false

17. true
18. true

19. −7
20. −2

21. −3
22. −19

23. true

24. False; the sum may be positive or negative. For example, $2 + (-1)$ is positive, but $2 + (-4)$ is negative.

25. −7; the sum $7 + (-7) = 0$, so 7 and −7 are opposites.

26. 23; the sum $23 + (-23) = 0$, so 23 and −23 are opposites.

27. 1; the sum $1 + (-1) = 0$, so 1 and −1 are opposites.

28. 0; the sum $0 + 0 = 0$, so 0 is its own opposite.

Lessons 1.4 and 1.5
Additional Practice

1. 1183
2. −1183

3. −7
4. 7

5. 1183
6. 7

7. −7
8. −1183

9. 7 and 8; 1 and 14

10. False; if two numbers are both positive, such as 4 and 8, the product is 32, which is not negative. If two numbers are both negative, such as −4 and −8, the product is 32, which is not negative.

11. True; for two numbers with different signs, such as −4 and 8 or 4 and −8, the product is −32, which is negative.

12. $(5 \cdot 82) \cdot 2 = (5 \cdot 2) \cdot 82 = 10 \cdot 82 = 820$

13. $29 \cdot 36 = (30 - 1) \cdot 36 =$ $30 \cdot 36 - 1 \cdot 36 = 1080 - 36 = 1044$

14. $18 \cdot 701 = 18 \cdot (700 + 1) =$ $18 \cdot 700 + 18 \cdot 1 =$ $12{,}600 + 18 = 12{,}618$

15. $22 \cdot 53 = 22 \cdot (50 + 3) =$ $22 \cdot 50 + 22 \cdot 3 = 1100 + 66 = 1166$

16. −73
17. 73

18. −1
19. −1

20. 12
21. 29

22. 42
23. 30

24. 18

Lessons 1.7 and 1.8
Additional Practice

1. Try $\frac{19}{32}$ in.; this is the next-smallest diameter, since $\frac{3}{4}$ was slightly too large.

Practice Workbook Answers *(continued)*

2. B   **3.** A

4. D   **5.** C

6. no   **7.** no

8. yes   **9.** yes

10. no   **11.** no

12. $\frac{3}{20}$ **13.** $-\frac{279}{100}$

14. $\frac{9}{2}$ **15.** $\frac{61}{100}$

16.

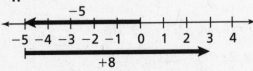

17. B   **18.** yes

19. no   **20.** yes

21. yes   **22.** no

23. no

Lessons 1.9 and 1.10
Additional Practice

1.

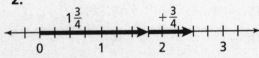

2.

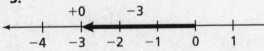

3.

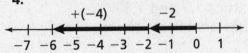

4.

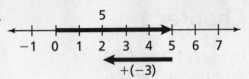

5.

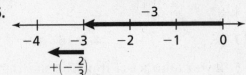

6.

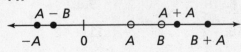

7. The upper arrow should have its tail point at 6 and its tip at 2.

8–11.

A − B   *A + A*

−*A*   0   *A*   *B*   *B + A*

12. 21   **13.** 9

14. 7   **15.** $\frac{3}{10}$

16. 9   **17.** $-\frac{5}{9}$

18. R   **19.** S

20. P   **21.** Q

Lessons 1.12 and 1.13
Additional Practice

1. 5555   **2.** 9876

3. 6783

4. length: $9\frac{2}{3}$ yd, 29 ft; width: $4\frac{1}{3}$ yd, 13 ft

5. $\frac{67}{60}$ **6.** 45

7. 79   **8.** 36

9–12. Answers may vary. Samples are given.

9. $\frac{3}{2}, \frac{5}{2}, \frac{-4}{2}$ **10.** $\frac{-3}{1}, \frac{-3}{4}, \frac{-1}{4}$

11. $\frac{1}{3}, \frac{1}{9}, \frac{1}{18}$ **12.** $\frac{1}{2}, \frac{1}{3}, \frac{-5}{6}$

13. $\frac{1}{50}$ **14.** $\frac{2}{15}$

15. $\frac{2}{11}$

16. Answers may vary. Sample: The sum is two times the first term. More specifically, if the denominator of the fourth term is the common denominator, then the numerators are 6, 3, 2, and 1.

Lessons 1.14 and 1.15
Additional Practice

1. a. Divide 1 million inches by 12 inches/foot.
   b. Divide the answer from part (a) by 5280 feet/mile; 16 miles

2.

	8
500	4000
30	240
7	56
	4296

3.

	6
700	4200
9	54
	4254

4.

	7
2,000	14,000
300	2,100
50	350
7	49
	16,499

5.

	3
10,000	30,000
4,000	12,000
10	30
2	6
	42,036

6. 4623

7. 5025

8. 7437

9. 8442

10. Answers may vary. Sample: To get the first two digits of the product, double the first factor. The last two digits of the product are the same as the first factor.

11. 49

12. 62

13. 135

14. No; $\frac{24}{48} = \frac{1}{2}$, which is not given by this method. $\frac{12}{24} = \frac{1}{2}$, which is not given by this method. $\frac{13}{39} = \frac{1}{3}$, which is not given by this method.

15. D

16. $\frac{1}{2}$

17. $\frac{13}{25}$

18. $\frac{105}{106}$

Chapter 2

Lessons 2.2 and 2.3
Additional Practice

1. a. 19 min   **b.** $(m + 7)$ min

2. a. III   **b.** I   **c.** II

3. Instructions for the expression $-2(x - 7) - 12$ would begin, "Choose any number. Subtract 7. Multiply by -2," which is different from the given instructions. The correct expression is $-2x - 7 - 12$ or $-2x - 19$.

4. a. -11 **b.** -63
   c. $-4(m + 5) - 3$ **d.** -23

5. a. 4   **b.** 4   **c.** 4   **d.** 4

6. a. 100   **b.** 4   **c.** $\frac{1}{2}$

7. a. When Kathy substituted for x in both evaluations, she subtracted 2 first rather than multiplying by 3.
   b. 13; 4

Practice Workbook Answers *(continued)*

Lessons 2.4 and 2.5
Additional Practice

1. a. No; the expression equals $3m - 7n$.
  b. No; the expression equals $-15mn$.
  c. yes

2. a. area: $5(12x - 7) = 60x - 35$;
    perimeter: $2(5) + 2(12x - 7) = 24x - 4$
  b. area: $13(-3x - 4) = -39x - 52$;
    perimeter: $2(13) + 2(-3x - 4) = -6x + 18$
  c. area: $8(5 + 7x) = 40 + 56x$;
    perimeter: $2(8) + 2(5 + 7x) = 14x + 26$

3. a. 3   **b.** -6 **c.** $-\frac{9}{10}$

  d. -1 **e.** $x - 1$

4. a. 28   **b.** 36   **c.** 45   **d.** 55
  e. Since n and $n + 1$ are consecutive numbers, one of them must be even. The product of an even number and an odd number is even, and is therefore evenly divisible by 2.

5. a. $5 \boxdot 3 = \frac{2(5)(3)}{5 + 3} = \frac{30}{8} = 3.75$

  b. $10 \boxdot 3 = \frac{2(10)(3)}{10 + 3} = \frac{60}{13}$

  c. yes; $a \boxdot b = \frac{2ab}{a + b} = \frac{2ba}{b + a} = b \boxdot a$

6. a. $7y + 35$ **b.** $y + 5$
  c. When $y = -5$, each expression is 0 because the common term in each product, $y + 5$, equals 0. Each multiplication result is 0, and if you add any number of zeros, you get 0.

7. a. 1st step: $m - 6$;
    2nd step: $5(m - 6)$ or $5m - 30$;
    3rd step: $5m - 30 + 100$ or $5m + 70$;
    4th step: $2(5m + 70)$ or $10m + 140$;
    5th step: $10m + 140 - 20$ or
        $10m + 120$;
    6th step: $\frac{10m + 120}{10}$ or $m + 12$
  b. Add 12 to the starting number.

Lessons 2.7 and 2.8
Additional Practice

1. a. Multiply by -5. Subtract 7.
    To reverse: Add 7. Divide by -5.
  b. Add 6. Divide by 3.
    To reverse: Multiply by 3.
    Subtract 6.
  c. Multiply by -4. Add 15.
    To reverse: Subtract 15.
    Divide by -4.

2. -3

3. Multiply both sides by 528. Add 1017 to each side.

4. a. 2   **b.** -1

5. -5

6. -90

7. 4

8. a. $\frac{4}{3}$ **b.** 7.5   **c.**

m	n
0	12
1	$\frac{32}{3}$
2	$\frac{28}{3}$
3	8
4	$\frac{20}{3}$
5	$\frac{16}{3}$
6	4

9. $\frac{11}{3}$

10. $-\frac{3}{11}$

11. $-\frac{11}{3}$

Practice Workbook Answers (continued)

Lessons 2.10 and 2.11
Additional Practice

1. 3
2. 4
3. −11
4. 5
5. −4
6. 7
7. 8
8. $-\frac{6}{5}$
9. 2
10. $\frac{5}{3}$
11. $\frac{10}{7}$

12. Same steps: Subtract x from each side. Subtract 3 from each side. Different steps: Divide each side by a different number.

13. Answers may vary. Sample: Add 23 to each side to get $17x = 32x + 71$. Subtract $32x$ from each side to get $-15x = 71$. Divide each side by −15 to get $x = -\frac{71}{15}$.

14. −8
15. $\frac{77}{6}$

16. a. Add 7 to each side.
b. Subtract 13 from each side.
c. Subtract $2x$ from each side.
d. Add 17 to each side.
e. Subtract 20 from each side.
f. Divide each side by 3.

17. Each solution is $\frac{37}{3}$; since all equations came about by applying the basic moves, they will all give the same answer for x.

18. a. 3 **b.** 3 **c.** 3
d. They all have the same solution. They are all the same basic equation $6x - 4 = 17 - x$, but the same number is added to or subtracted from both sides.

Lessons 2.12 and 2.13
Additional Practice

1. no solution
2. all real numbers
3. 2
4. −1
5. no solution
6. all real numbers
7. 2
8. 1
9. 5
10. −2
11. $-\frac{1}{2}$
12. $-\frac{1}{2}$

13. a. Subtract $5x$ from each side and then add $3y$ to each side.
b. Add $3y$ to each side.
c. Add $3y$ to each side and then divide each side by 5.

14. $\frac{6}{5}$
15. −13
16. −1
17. 14
18. $-\frac{1}{3}$
19. 2
20. −3
21. 19
22. 3
23. 1
24. $\frac{1}{5}$

Lessons 2.15 and 2.16
Additional Practice

1. a. no **b.** yes **c.** no
d. $23(18 + d) = 575$ or $23(18 + d) - 360 = 215$
e. 7 days

2. 450 mi

3. $450

4. 174

5. a. $\frac{2}{5}$ **b.** $\frac{3}{5}$ **c.** $1 - w$

6. 20 lb

7. 880 cans

8. a. If you plug $x = 5$ into the equation $2(5 - 3x) = -5(3x + 7)$, you get $-20 = -110$, which is a false statement. So, $x = 5$ is not the correct solution.

  b. In the fourth step, Victor added $-6x + 15x$ incorrectly and got $-9x$. The correct step is $10 + 9x = -35$.

  c. The remaining steps should be as follows:
$$10 + 9x = -35$$
$$9x = -45$$
$$x = -5$$

Lesson 2.17 Additional Practice

1. $a = b - 3; b = a + 3$

2. a. No; $7(4) - 3(-5) = 28 + 15$ equals 43, not 42.

  b. 7

  c. Answers may vary. Sample: $(0, -14), (3, -7), (6, 0)$

3. a. $2\ell + 2w$

  b. The left side, $2\ell + 2w$, is an expression for the perimeter. The right side, $4(\ell - w + 7)$, is a translation for the description of the perimeter given in the exercise.

  c. $\ell = 3w - 14$ **d.** 10 in.; 36 in.

4. a. 120 pairs of women's shoes

  b. No; for 150 pairs of women's shoes, the store would have made $150 \cdot \$18 = \$2700$, which leaves $\$2880 - \$2700 = \$180$ for men's shoes. However, $\$180$ is not evenly divisible by $\$24$ per pair, so the store cannot have sold 150 pairs of women's shoes.

  c. 69 pairs of men's shoes, 68 pairs of women's shoes

5. a. $y = -\frac{4}{7}x + 8$ **b.** $x = -\frac{7}{4}y + 14$

6. a. $y = -\frac{5}{7}x + \frac{29}{7}$ **b.** $x = -\frac{7}{5}y + \frac{29}{5}$

Chapter 3

Lesson 3.2 Additional Practice

1. The new point is below the original point.

2. Add a positive value to the x-coordinate. Leave the y-coordinate the same.

3. a. $(-4, -6)$; the point is reflected across the x-axis.

  b. $(4, 6)$; the point is reflected across the y-axis.

  c. $(4, -6)$; the point is reflected across the origin, or rotated 180°.

4. a.

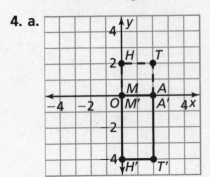

Answers may vary. Sample: The shape is reflected across the x-axis. It has the same horizontal length and twice the vertical height as the original.

  b.

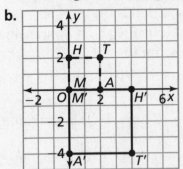

Answers may vary. Sample: The square is rotated 90° clockwise and the length of each side is doubled.

Practice Workbook Answers (continued)

5. Yes; answers may vary. Samples:

Any oblique line that contains the origin passes through exactly two quadrants. ($y = 2x$ passes through Quadrants I and III; $y = -x$ passes through Quadrants II and IV.)

Any vertical or horizontal line that does not contain the origin passes through exactly two quadrants. ($y = 5$ passes through Quadrants I and II; $x = -3$ passes through Quadrants II and III.)

6. Yes; the x-axis ($y = 0$) and the y-axis ($x = 0$) pass through no quadrants.

7. The triangle shifts 3 units right and 4 units up.

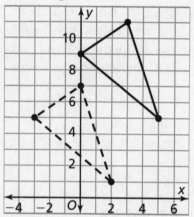

8. The rectangle moves 4 units down.

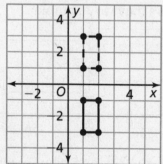

9. The square becomes a rectangle; the horizontal side is twice as long and the vertical side is three times as long.

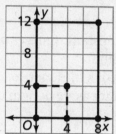

10. The triangle is reflected across the x-axis and rotated 90° clockwise. Then the vertical height is doubled.

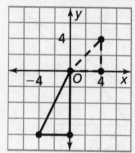

Lessons 3.3 and 3.4
Additional Practice

1. a. "Find the two numbers that are 5 units away from 11." The solutions are 16 and 6.
  b. "Find the two numbers that are 12 units away from −3." The solutions are 9 and −15.
  c. "Find the numbers that are less than 3 units away from 4." The solution is $1 < x < 7$.

2. a. 10 **b.** 13 **c.** 17

3. Answers may vary. Sample:
  a. $|x| = 17$ **b.** $|x - 11| = 4$
  c. $|x - 6| = 0$ **d.** $|x + 8| = 3$
  e. $|x - 3| = 5$ **f.** $|x| = -1$

4. a. 15, −15 **b.** 5, −5
  c. 1.5, −1.5 **d.** $\pm\frac{1}{20}$

Practice Workbook Answers (continued)

e. You can divide to solve the equation and write "±" in front of the quotient.

5. Answers may vary. Sample:
  a. Fred reads a constant number of pages per minute.
  b. The wingspan of a bird increases at a constant rate as the length of the bird grows.

6. a. B and C   **b.** C and D
  c. A and B

7. a.   **Sam's and Beth's Exercise**

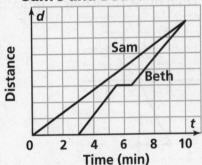

b.   **Cathy's and Dave's Walk**

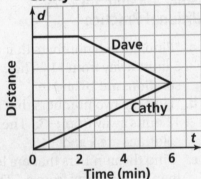

Lessons 3.6 and 3.7
Additional Practice

1. 3.15×10^5

2. a. Double each element in the original set. The mean and median also double.
  b. Subtract 2 from each element in the original set. The mean and median also decrease by 2.

3. a.

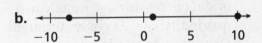

b.

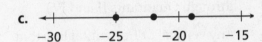

c.

d.

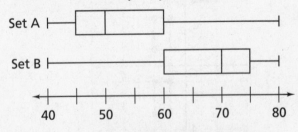

e. The distance from the mean to each of the two points is the same.

4. C

5. Answers may vary. Sample: The wide difference between the median and mean age may come from the fact that there are likely to be a number of parents at the party. It only takes one parent to increase the mean.

6. C

7. a. 12 cities
  b. The number of cities is the same.
  c. 77°F
  d. 46°F and 52°F

Lessons 3.8 and 3.9
Additional Practice

1. a. Answers may vary. Sample:

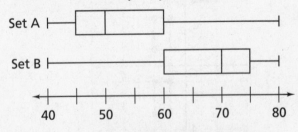

b. Yes; see the box-and-whisker plot from part (a).

2. B

Practice Workbook Answers *(continued)*

3. All of the new car prices are at least as great as the median used car price.

Car Selling Prices

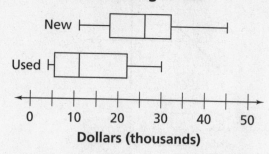

4. a.

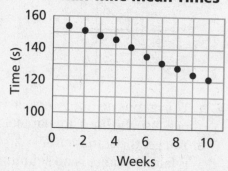

b. 100–110 seconds

5. a.

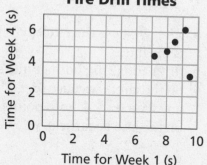

b. Yes; there is a general trend up and to the right. It shows that most of the Week 4 times are about 3 minutes faster than the Week 1 times.

c. Yes; the point (9.5, 3.2), corresponding to School D, is an outlier. Its Week 4 time is about 6 minutes less than its Week 1 time.

Lesson 3.11 Additional Practice

1. a. Answers may vary. Sample:
$(-3, -1)$, $(-3, 0)$, $(-3, 1)$, $(-3, 2)$, $(-3, 3)$, $(-3, 4)$

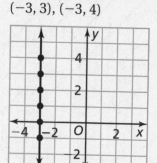

b. A line parallel to the y-axis and 3 units to the right of it; see part (a) for graph.

2. a. no; yes; no; yes
b. Answers may vary. Samples:
$(1, 1)$, $(4, 2)$, $(4, -2)$, $(9, 3)$

3. a. $h = -5$ **b.** $v = 3$

4. a. on neither **b.** on v
c. on h **d.** on both
e. on neither

5. a. $(2, -1)$, $(2, 0)$, $(2, 1)$, $(2, 2)$
b. $(-1, -4)$, $(0, -4)$, $(1, -4)$, $(2, -4)$
c. $a = 3$
d. $b = -4$
e.

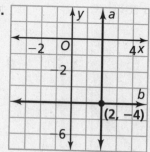

6. a. Answers may vary. Sample: $(0, -9)$, $(4, -6)$, $(8, -3)$, $(12, 0)$, $(16, 3)$
b. Answers may vary. Sample:
$(0, 0)$, $(0, 1)$, $(1, 0)$, $(2, 0)$, $(0, 2)$

CME Project • *Algebra 1 Teaching Resources*

Practice Workbook Answers *(continued)*

7. a–f.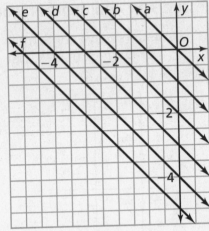

g. In each case, the y in the first equation is replaced with $(y + n)$, with n being a number that increases by 1 in each equation.

h. The graphs are parallel lines that shift down 1 unit for each increase of the number that is added to y. Adding a larger number to y moves the graph lower.

i. The graph of $y + 10 = -x$ is parallel to the other graphs and would cross the y-axis at $(0, -10)$. In other words, it is the first graph shifted 10 units down.

Lessons 3.12 and 3.13
Additional Practice

1. B

2. a. IV **b.** I **c.** II **d.** III

3. a.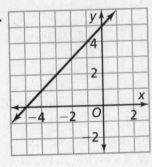

b.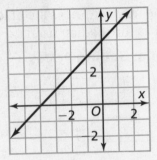

c.

4. a. The graphs do not intersect because the lines are parallel.

b. You get the statement $7 = 2$, which is false, so there is no solution.

5. Answers may vary. Sample:

$$y = -\tfrac{1}{2}x;\ x + y = 4$$

6. a. $x^2 + y^2 = 4$ is the circle; $x + y = 2$ is the line.

b. $(0, 2)$ and $(2, 0)$; both points are on the circle because $0^2 + 2^2 = 4$ and $2^2 + 0^2 = 4$. Both points are on the line because $0 + 2 = 2$ and $2 + 0 = 2$.

7. a. $(-3, 0)$ **b.** $(-3, 1)$ **c.** $(-3, 2)$
 d. $(-3, 3)$ **e.** $(-3, 4)$ **f.** $(-3, 5)$
 g. $(-3, 6)$ **h.** $(-3, 7)$ **i.** $(-3, 8)$
 j. $(-3, 9)$
 k. The x-coordinate is always -3. The y-coordinate is the value given in the equation.

Practice Workbook Answers (continued)

Lesson 3.15 Additional Practice

1. a. no   **b.** no   **c.** yes
     d. yes   **e.** yes   **f.** no

2. a. yes   **b.** yes   **c.** yes
     d. yes   **e.** no   **f.** yes

3. a.

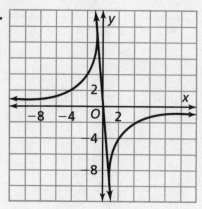

b. There are 2 points of intersection, $(-1, 8)$ and $(1, -8)$.

4. a. (p, q) is on the graph, so $pq = 48$.
For $(-p, -q)$, the product $(-p)(-q) = pq = 48$, so $(-p, -q)$ is on the graph.
For $(-q, -p)$, the product $(-q)(-p) = qp = pq = 48$, so $(-q, -p)$ is on the graph.

b. $(4, 12)$, $\left(\frac{1}{2}p, 2q\right)$, $\left(5q, \frac{1}{5}p\right)$

5. a. \$45   **b.** \$2.25   **c.** $c = 2.25b$

6. a. 8 songs   **b.** \$30.25   **c.** \$60.50

d.

Cost of Downloads

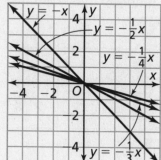

Cost (dollars) vs. Number of Songs

e. $c = 2.75s$

7. a. For $(3, 6)$, $6 = 2(3)$ and $(3)(6) = 18$, so $(3, 6)$ is on both graphs.
For $(-3, -6)$, $-6 = 2(-3)$ and $(-3)(-6) = 18$, so $(-3, -6)$ is on both graphs.

b.

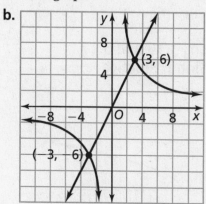

8. a–d.

e. $y = -5x$ is the steepest graph, while $y = -x$ is the flattest. As the number multiplied by x becomes more negative, the graph becomes downwardly steeper. All graphs still pass through the origin.

9. a–d.

e. $y = -x$ is the steepest graph, while $y = -\frac{1}{4}x$ is the flattest. As the number multiplied by x becomes less negative, the graph becomes flatter. All graphs still pass through the origin.

Lessons 3.16 and 3.17
Additional Practice

1. a. $x \geq -4$, $y \geq 0$

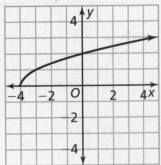

b. $x \leq 0$, $y \geq 0$

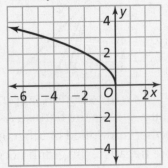

2. D

3. a. 2 points of intersection

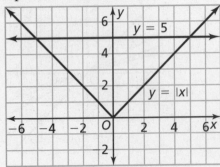

b. 2 points of intersection

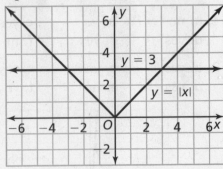

c. 1 point of intersection

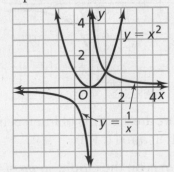

d. 1 point of intersection

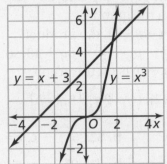

e. 2 points of intersection

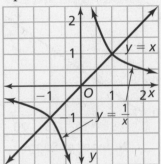

f. 2 points of intersection

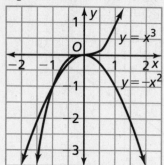

4. a. $y = x^2$ shifted 1 unit right

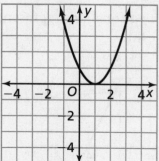

b. $y = x^2$ shifted 1 unit right and 2 units down

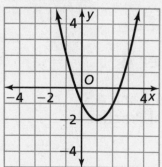

c. $y = x^3$ shifted 2 units down

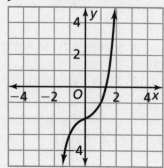

d. $y = x^3$ shifted 3 units right and 2 units down

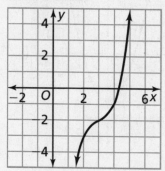

e. $y = \sqrt{x}$ shifted 5 units right

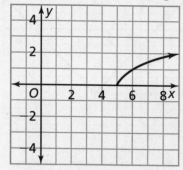

f. $y = \sqrt{x}$ shifted 5 units left

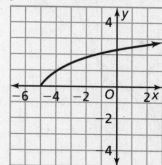

g. see parts (a)–(f)

5. a. $y = (x - 3)^2$

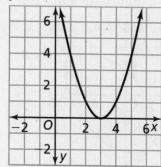

b. $(y + 3) = x^2$

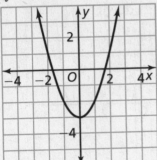

c. $(y + 4) = |x - 3|$

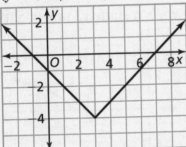

6. a–c.

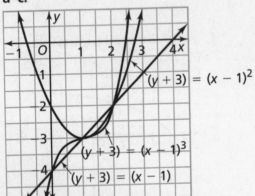

7. $M = -1$

8. The new graph is the original graph shifted 2 units right and 1 unit down.

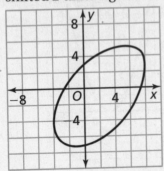

9. a. The two equations represent the same line.

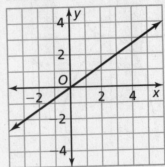

b. The two equations represent the same line.

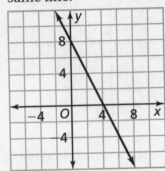

10. $(3, 2)$

Chapter 4

Lessons 4.2 and 4.3
Additional Practice

1. a. $-\frac{5}{3}$ **b.** $-\frac{1}{3}$

c. $-\frac{1}{3}$ **d.** 0

e. undefined   **f.** $\frac{8}{5}$

2. a–g. Answers may vary. Samples are given.
a. $Q(-1, 10)$ **b.** $Q(-1, 2)$
c. $Q(-1, 3)$ **d.** $Q(2, 5)$
e. $Q(-3, 2)$ **f.** $Q(0, 6)$
g. $Q(10, 1)$ or $Q(-14, 11)$

Practice Workbook Answers *(continued)*

3. a. The two points are on a horizontal line.
  b. One point is below and to the right of the other point.
  c. One point is above and to the right of the other point.
  d. The two points are on a vertical line.

4. a.

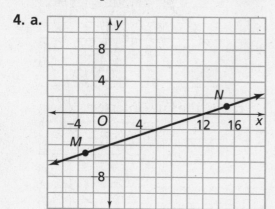

  b. $\frac{1}{3}$

  c. $m(M, R) = \frac{1}{3}$; $m(N, R) = \frac{1}{3}$

5. a. 10 hours
  b. 1 hour and 15 minutes
  c. 1 hour, 6 minutes, and 40 seconds

6. a. A and B **b.** B and C
  c. C and D
  d. 325 gallons; 25 hours; 13 gal/h

Lesson 4.4 Additional Practice

1. Q, R, S

2. Answers may vary. Sample:
$$\frac{y - 5}{x + 3} = -\frac{4}{3}$$

3. a–f. Answers may vary. Samples are given.
  a. (5, 2), (0, 17), (1, 14); collinear
  b. (0, 4), (−3, 3), (6, 6); collinear
  c. (0, −5), (2, −1), (1, −3); collinear
  d. (0, −7), (−14, 0), (2, −8); collinear

  e. (0, 1), $\left(1, -\frac{1}{3}\right)$, $\left(2, \frac{1}{9}\right)$; not collinear
  f. (−1, −2), (0, 0), (1, −2); not collinear

4. b, f, h

5. D

6. a. yes   **b.** no
  c. no   **d.** yes
  e. In parts (a) and (b), points X, Y, and Z are on the line $x = y$. In parts (c) and (d), X, Y, and Z are on the line $x = -y$.

7. a. yes   **b.** no
  c. yes   **d.** no
  e. In parts (a) and (b), the points that are of the form $(x, x + 3)$ are collinear. In parts (c) and (d), the points that are of the form $(x, x - 10)$ are collinear.

Lesson 4.6 Additional Practice

1. a. No; the equation contains an x^2 term and a y^2 term, and cannot be rewritten in the form $ax + by = c$.

  b. Yes; slope $= -\frac{5}{4}$; the line crosses axes at (0, 20) and (16, 0).

  c. Yes; slope $= \frac{4}{5}$; the line crosses axes at (0, 15) and (−18.75, 0).

  d. Yes; slope $= -\frac{1}{4}$; the line crosses axes at (0, −10) and (−40, 0).

  e. No; the equation contains an xy term, and cannot be rewritten in the form $ax + by = c$.

  f. Yes; slope $= \frac{2}{3}$; the line crosses axes at (0, −6) and (9, 0).

2. Let the x-coordinate of a point P be p. Substituting p in the equation of the line, you get $y = -5p + 7$. So $P(p, -5p + 7)$ is on the graph of $5x + y = 7$.

You can find a second point Q on the line using the same method to get $Q(q, -5q + 7)$.

Then find the slope between points P and Q.

$$m(P, Q) = \frac{(-5p + 7) - (-5q + 7)}{p - q}$$
$$= \frac{-5p + 7 + 5q - 7}{p - q}$$
$$= \frac{-5p + 5q}{p - q}$$
$$= \frac{-5(p - q)}{p - q}$$
$$= -5$$

So, no matter what p and q are, the slope of the line that contains P and Q will always be -5.

3. a. -6 **b.** $-\frac{5}{6}$ **c.** 1

    d. $\frac{5}{13}$ **e.** $\frac{5}{13}$ **f.** 1

4. a. 296 words   **b.** 481 words
    c. D

5. C

6. $y + 6 = -2(x - 7)$; Answers may vary. Sample: $(0, 8)$; No, every point on the line must satisfy the equation.

7. a. Yes, the lines intersect.

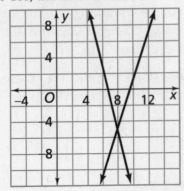

b. Yes, the lines intersect.

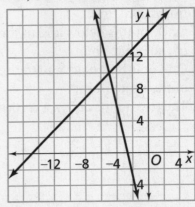

c. Yes, the lines intersect.

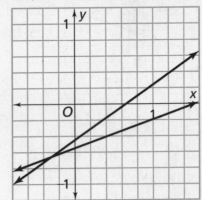

d. The lines intersect at point (a, b) for equations that are in the form $(y - b) = m(x - a)$, and m is not the same in both equations.

Lessons 4.7 and 4.8
Additional Practice

1. a. $y + 2 = -2(x - 5)$

    b. $y - 4 = \frac{1}{3}(x + 3)$

    c. $y + 2 = -\frac{2}{3}(x - 8)$

    d. $y + 7 = -\frac{2}{5}(x + 4)$

    e. $y - 7 = 0$

    f. $x = -8$

2. a.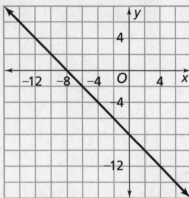

b.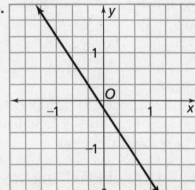

c.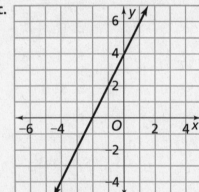

d.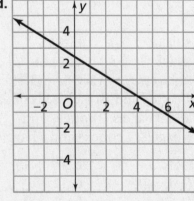

e.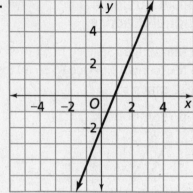

f.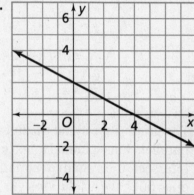

3. a. A   **b.** 15 hours

4. a. I, III
  b. II, Kristin starts first.
  c. In graph I, Kristin is faster.
    In graph II, Vicky is faster.
  d. Kristin: $y = 15x$;
    Vicky: $y = 30x - 300$

5. a.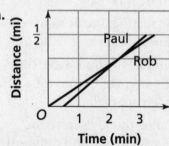

b. Paul took $3\frac{1}{2}$ minutes. Rob took
  $3\frac{1}{4}$ minutes. Rob finished first.

Practice Workbook Answers *(continued)*

Lessons 4.10 and 4.11
Additional Practice

1. a. Messenger Service B; $1 less
 b. Messenger Service A; $6.50 less
 c. 12 miles

2. a. no solution
 b.

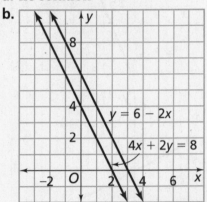

The graph shows that the lines are parallel. Since parallel lines do not intersect, the system of equations does not have a solution.

3. a. $(22, 510)$
 b. No solution; the lines have the same slope and different y-intercepts, so the lines are parallel.

4. a. Parallel; the lines have the same slope of 0.4 and different y-intercepts.
 b. Intersecting; the lines have different slopes.
 c. Identical; the lines have the same slope of $-\frac{3}{2}$ and the same y-intercept of $\frac{5}{2}$.
 d. Parallel; the lines have the same slope of $\frac{2}{3}$ and different y-intercepts.

5. a. $y + 3 = -\frac{5}{6}(x - 12)$
 b. $y + 5 = \frac{2}{3}(x + 6)$
 c. $y + 4 = -\frac{2}{3}(x - 1)$
 d. $x = -2$
 e. $y = -11$

6. a. $k = -8$ **b.** $k = -8$
 c. $k = -8$ **d.** $k = -8$
 e. $k = -8$
 f. Answers may vary. Sample: If the graph of $y = mx + k$ contains $(0, b)$, then $k = q$.

7. a. $k = 40$ **b.** $k = 48$
 c. $k = 56$ **d.** $k = 800$
 e. $k = 8q$
 f. Answers may vary. Sample: If the graph of $y = mx + k$ contains $(a, 0)$, then $k = -ma$.

Lesson 4.12 Additional Practice

1. a. $(5, -2)$ **b.** $(-3, -4)$
 c. $(5, 13)$ **d.** $\left(\frac{2}{3}, \frac{4}{3}\right)$
 e. $\left(2, \frac{2}{5}\right)$ **f.** $(12, -8)$

2. a. $2.50   **b.** $1.50

3. a. $P(-2, 6)$ **b.** $x = -2$
 c. $y = 6$ **d.** $-4x + 7y = 50$

4. $y - 8 = -3(x + 5),\ y - 8 = \frac{3}{4}(x + 5)$

5. Answers may vary. Sample:
$y = \frac{3}{5}x + 2$

6. a. $2.25   **b.** $.75
 c. $3.00   **d.** $1.50
 e. Answers may vary. Samples: 1 coffee and 10 bagels, 2 coffees and 8 bagels, 3 coffees and 6 bagels, 4 coffees and 4 bagels

7. a. $(4, 9)$ **b.** $(-6, 38)$
 c. $(-3, -2)$ **d.** $(2, -6)$
 e. $(1, 5)$ **f.** $(6, -3)$

Practice Workbook Answers *(continued)*

8. a. $(-2, 6)$ **b.** $\left(\frac{1}{2}, \frac{2}{3}\right)$

c. no solution

Lesson 4.14 Additional Practice

1. a. $x < \frac{11}{5}$

b. $x < -8$ or $x > 5$

c. $-8 < x < 10$

d. $x \leq -2.2$ or $x \geq -1.8$

e. no solution

f. $x < -1$ or $x > 1$

2. a. $x \leq -1.25$

b.

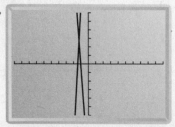

The image does not immediately give any useful information about the intersection of the lines since the two lines are close together. Adjusting the graphing calculator's window to find the intersection may help, but it is easier to solve this inequality using algebra.

3. a.

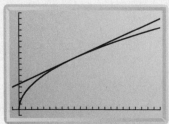

When $\frac{x+9}{2} < \sqrt{9x}$, the graph of $y = \frac{x+9}{2}$ must be below the graph of $y = \sqrt{9x}$. Testing values near the intersection at $x = 9$ shows that the line is higher than or equal to the square root for all values. Therefore, there is no solution to $\frac{x+9}{2} < \sqrt{9x}$.

4. Wherever the graph is on or below the x-axis, that value of x is a solution to $x^2 + 5x + 4 \leq 0$. Since the graph crosses $y = 0$ at $x = -1$ and $x = -4$, the solution is $-4 \leq x \leq -1$.

5. a.

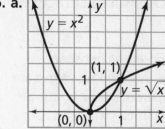

b. $x < 0$ or $x > 1$

c.

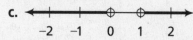

6. a.

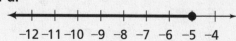

b.

c. Combine these number lines by including only numbers that are part of both number lines.

d. All real numbers; the solution is the entire number line.

7. a.

b.

c.

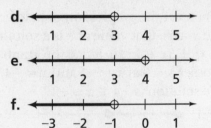

d. (number line with points 1 2 3 4 5, open circle at 3)

e. (number line with points 1 2 3 4 5, open circle at 4)

f. (number line with points −3 −2 −1 0 1, open circle at −1)

Lesson 4.15 Additional Practice

1. D

2. a. The differences between consecutive income values are not constant, so the points are not on a line.

b. Yes, there is a linear trend.

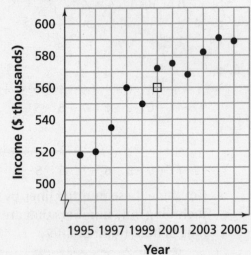

c. (2000, 560), see plot in part (b); yes

3. a.

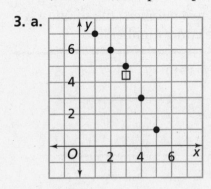

b.

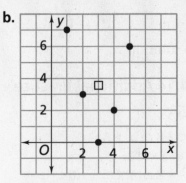

c.

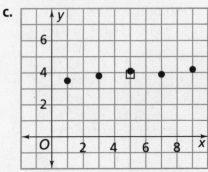

4. a. (3, 4.4)   **b.** (3, 3.6)

c. (5, 3.9)

5. a. Answers may vary. Sample:

$$y - 4.4 = -\frac{3}{2}(x - 3)$$

b. not a linear trend

c. Answers may vary. Sample:

$$y - 3.9 = \frac{0.7}{8}(x - 5)$$

6. a.

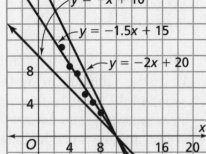

$y = -x + 10$

$y = -1.5x + 15$

$y = -2x + 20$

b. C

Chapter 5

Lessons 5.2 and 5.3
Additional Practice

1. 16 weeks   **2.** 30.6 weeks

3. 47.3 weeks   **4.** 52.1 weeks

5. 57 feet   **6.** 1050 feet

7. 5280 feet   **8.** 30,000 feet

9. a. $99,000   **b.** $137,500
      c. $288,750

10. $55h$ dollars   **11.** $32,670

12. a. Yes; each page has a fixed number
      of words.
    b. Yes; if the area of a square is
      known, then there is a single value
      for the side of the square and for
      the perimeter of the square.
    c. No; different rectangles may
      have the same area, and different
      rectangles may have different
      perimeters.

13. Yes; time is the independent variable
and temperature is the dependent
variable.

14. 1

15. Again, the result is 1. For any number
greater than zero, the square root of
that number is between that number
and 1. After taking square roots 20
or 30 times, the result is so close to 1
that the calculator displays it as 1.

16. a. The outputs alternate. The outputs
      are −0.06, 0.06, −0.06, 0.06, −0.06,
      0.06, and so on.
    b. Answers may vary. Sample:
      Let $x = 0.02$. The outputs are
      −0.02, 0.02, −0.02, 0.02, −0.02,
      0.02, and so on.

c. The outputs are the same in that
they alternate between a negative
and a positive value. The outputs
are different because the number
values are different.

Lesson 5.4 Additional Practice

1. functions h and k **2.** function j

3. 14   **4.** −15

5. none

6. Check students' work; the output is
always 2.

7. $x \rightarrow x+1 \rightarrow x^2+2x+1 \rightarrow x^2+2x \rightarrow$
$x+2 \rightarrow 2$

8. 8, 12, 12   **9.** 5, 1, 11

10. 25   **11.** 48

12. 13   **13.** 2

14. 7   **15.** 32

16. 2   **17.** 1

18. 12   **19.** 12

20. 7

Lessons 5.5 and 5.6
Additional Practice

1. all real numbers   **2.** all real numbers

3. all real numbers except −3

4. all real numbers greater than or
equal to −3

5. all real numbers   **6.** all real numbers

7. 11   **8.** 5   **9.** $\frac{1}{2}$

10. 13   **11.** 4   **12.** $\frac{3}{2x+5}$

13. Yes; it passes the vertical line test.

14. No; it fails the vertical line test.

15. Yes; it passes the vertical line test.

16.

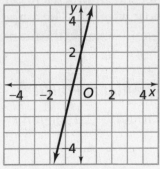

17.

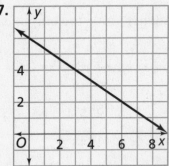

18.

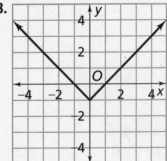

19.

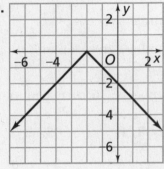

20.

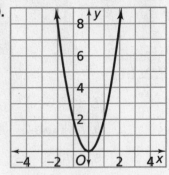

21.

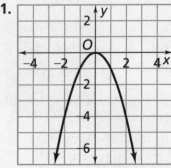

22. a. $f(x) = 10x + 50$
b. $110

23. a. $f(x) = 9.50x - 209$
b. $19
c. 44 shirts

Lesson 5.8 Additional Practice

1. 8799 ft³; 15,084 ft³ for each 100 feet of depth, the oil company removes 1257 ft³ of earth, so $(7)(1257) = 8799$ and $(12)(1257) = 15,084$.

2. $V = \dfrac{1257D}{100}$

3. 410 ft

4. In Table A, the missing values in the output column are −2, −3, −4, −5, and −6. In Table B, the missing values in the difference column are 1, 3, 5, and 7. In Table C, the missing values in the output column are 0, 5, 10, 15, and 20.

Practice Workbook Answers (continued)

5. Table A: $f(x) = -x - 3$;
Table C: $f(x) = 2.5x$

6. B

7.

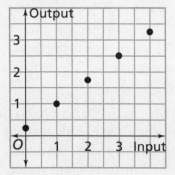

8. $f(x) = \frac{3}{4}x + \frac{1}{4}$

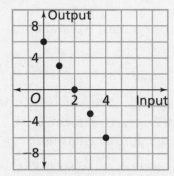

9. $f(x) = -3x + 6$

10.

Lesson 5.9 Additional Practice

1. Rule 1   Rule 2

x	y
0	1
1	2
2	4
3	8

x	y
0	1
1	2
2	4
3	7

The tables are not the same, so the rules do not define the same function.

2. Rules 1 and 2

x	y
0	2
1	1
2	0
3	-1

The tables are the same, so the rules define the same function.

3. $v(n) = \begin{cases} 30,000, & \text{if } n = 0 \\ 0.85 \cdot f(n-1), & \text{if } n > 0 \end{cases}$

At the end of 5 years, the car is worth about $13,311.

4.

x	y
0	-50
1	-42
2	-34
3	-26
4	-18
5	-10
6	-2
7	6
8	14

5. The difference between consecutive output values is a constant 8. Yes, the linear function $f(x) = 8x - 50$ can generate the table.

CME Project • *Algebra 1 Teaching Resources*

Practice Workbook Answers *(continued)*

6. 16 hours; solving $75 = 8x - 50$ gives $x = 15.625$. Then round to a whole number.

7.

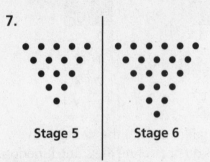

Stage	Stage 5	Stage 6

Stage	1	2	3	4	5	6
Number of Dots Added	1	2	3	4	5	6
Total Number of Dots	1	3	6	10	15	21

8. $f(n) = \begin{cases} 1, & \text{if } n = 1 \\ f(n-1) + n, & \text{if } n > 1 \end{cases}$

9. not a linear function

Input	Output
0	5
1	15
2	45
3	135
4	405
5	1215

10. $f(x) = -3x + 4$

Input	Output
0	4
1	1
2	-2
3	-5
4	-8
5	-11

Lesson 5.11 Additional Practice

1.

Cost Without Membership → Multiply by 0.15. → Discount → Subtract. → Cost With Membership

2. $M(b) = 0.85b$

3. $b > 200$; membership becomes worthwhile when the amount of the discount exceeds the cost of membership. This happens when

$$b - M(b) > 30$$
$$b - 0.85b > 30$$
$$0.15b > 30$$
$$b > 200$$

When Monica spends more than $200 bowling, the membership saves her money.

4. $660; if twice as many people bowled duckpins, then 120 people bowled duckpins and 60 people bowled candlepins. The total spent would be $120 \cdot \$3 + 60 \cdot \$5 = \$360 + \$300 = \$660$.

5. 110 duckpin games, 70 candlepin games

6. 1575; $1312.50

7. $350 for savings; $500 for emergencies; $380 each for entertainment, food, clothing, and further education.

8. She earned $200 \cdot \$30$ or $6000. She paid 55%, or $3300, for taxes and rent. She had $2700 left. She saved 15% of the remainder, or $405, and put away $500 for emergencies. She had $1795 left. Dividing the remainder into four equal amounts leaves about $450 for each of entertainment, food, clothing, and further education.

9. 15 and 23

10. 7, 13, 19, 25

Lesson 5.12 Additional Practice

1.

Input	Output
0	40,000
1	30,000
2	22,500
3	16,875
4	12,656
5	9,492
6	7,119
7	5,339
8	4,005

2. The output for $n = 0$ is 40,000. The output for each subsequent value of n is three fourths times the value of the previous output.

3. $W(n) = \begin{cases} 40,000, & \text{if } n = 0 \\ \frac{3}{4}W(n-1), & \text{if } n > 0 \end{cases}$

4. exponential rule; $W(n) = 40,000 \cdot \left(\frac{3}{4}\right)^n$

5. on the 37th day

6. For both rules, the first 10 outputs are 10, 5, −5, −10, −5, 5, 10, 5, −5, and −10.

7. Both rules state that the first two outputs, $r(1)$ and $r(2)$, are 10 and 5. Both rules also state that to get each subsequent output, which is $r(n)$ for $n > 2$, take the previous output, $r(n-1)$, and subtract the output before it, $r(n-2)$.

8. The outputs are −5, 4, 9, 5, −4, −9, −5, 4, 9, 5, −4, −9, . . . The pattern repeats after 6 outputs. The 150th output is the same as the 6th output because 6 divides into 150 evenly. So, the 155th output is the same as the 5th output, which is −4.

9. a. The first output is the value N. To find each subsequent output, square the previous output, multiply that by 2, and then add the value N.

b. When $N = 2$, the first outputs are 2, 10, 202, 81, 610, . . . The output values increase. When $N = 0$, the outputs are 0, 0, 0, 0, . . . The outputs remain the same. When $N = -1$, the outputs are −1, 1, 1, 1, . . . In the long run, the outputs remain the same.

10. $f(n) = 2n - 5$ **11.** $h(n) = -n - 7$

12. $g(n) = -3n + 8$ **13.** $k(n) = pn - q$

Chapter 6

Lessons 6.2 and 6.3 Additional Practice

1. a. $x^4 y^2$ **b.** $9a^3 b^3$ **c.** $3m^9$
   d. $32a^8$ **e.** $72x^5$ **f.** $24x^6$

2. a. 4   **b.** 6   **c.** 2
   d. 3   **e.** 4   **f.** 1

3. a. 5 in.   **b.** 6.25 in.
   c. 15.26 in.   **d.** $(4 \cdot 1.25^n)$ in.

4. a. 4.8 in.   **b.** 3.84 in.
   c. 1.57 in.   **d.** $(6 \cdot 0.8^n)$ in.

5. a. yes   **b.** no   **c.** yes
   d. no   **e.** yes

   f. $\left(-\frac{1}{x}\right)^n = -\left(\frac{1}{x}\right)^n$ is an identity if n is odd.

Practice Workbook Answers (continued)

6. a. No; the expression equals 7^7.

   b. No; the expression equals 7^6.

   c. No; the expression equals 7^{14}.

   d. Yes; the expression equals $\frac{7^{10}}{7^2} = 7^8$.

7. a. m^{15} **b.** m^{15} **c.** m^{81}
   d. m^3 **e.** m^5

8. a. Divide by 3 to get the next term;
      27, 9, 3

   b. Divide by 10 to get the next term;
      10, 1, 0.1

   c. Divide by 8 to get the next term;
      $1, \frac{1}{8}, \frac{1}{64}$

   d. Multiply by 5 to get the next term;
      $\frac{1}{5}, 1, 5$

   e. Divide by $\frac{1}{3}$ to get the next term;
      1, 3, 9

   f. Divide by 5 to get the next term;
      $5^2, 5, 1$

Lessons 6.4 and 6.5
Additional Practice

1. a. 1   **b.** 5   **c.** 3

2. a. No; the expression equals 4^{-2}.
   b. Yes; you can rewrite the expression
      as $4^{(-6)+(-2)}$, so it equals 4^{-8}.
   c. No; the expression equals 4^{15}.
   d. Yes; you can rewrite the expression
      as $4^{(2)\cdot(-4)}$, so it equals 4^{-8}.
   e. Yes; you can rewrite the expression
      as $4^{(5-13)}$, so it equals 4^{-8}.
   f. Yes; you can rewrite the expression
      as $(4^{-1})^8$ or 4^{-8}.
   g. No; the expression equals 4^8.
   h. No; the expression equals 4^8.

3. a. p^5 **b.** p^{-30} **c.** p^{-6} **d.** p^2

4. a. 1   **b.** 4   **c.** 13
   d. 40   **e.** 121
   f. Each sum is the previous sum plus
      the next power of 3.

5. a. 1×10^6 **b.** 4.75×10^4
   c. 5.12×10^8 **d.** 2.02×10^5
   e. 2.31×10^{-3} **f.** 3.579×10^{-5}
   g. 1.64×10^{13} **h.** 1.08×10^9
   i. 2.17×10^6

6. a. 253,000
   b. 410,320,000,000
   c. 0.0000159
   d. 0.0000000472
   e. 7.2
   f. 5,060,000,000,000

7. a. mean: 24,032; median: 9.8×10^3
   b. mean: 57,973; median: 28.2×10^3

8. a. 1.25×10^{23} **b.** 1.6×10^{19}
   c. 3.844×10^{11} **d.** 2×10^7
   e. 3.1×10^6 **f.** 1.3×10^3

Lessons 6.7 and 6.8
Additional Practice

1. 17, 19, 23

2. a. $\sqrt{30}$ **b.** $\sqrt{55}$
   c. $\sqrt{66}$ **d.** no
   e. $(mnp)^2 = 330$

3. a. 1   **b.** 1

4. a. 1 cm   **b.** 2 cm
   c. $\sqrt{2}$ cm   **d.** $\sqrt{3}$ cm

5. a. no; 3 and 4   **b.** no; 3 and 4
   c. yes   **d.** no; 4 and 5
   e. no; 5 and 6   **f.** 37

6. a. $2\sqrt{6}$ **b.** $10\sqrt{5}$
   c. $63\sqrt{21}$

7. a. 3   **b.** 6
   c. 1   **d.** 5

8. $\frac{\sqrt{15}}{\sqrt{5}}, \sqrt{3 \cdot 4}, \sqrt{15}, \sqrt{15} + \sqrt{5},$
   $\sqrt{15 \cdot 5}$

Practice Workbook Answers *(continued)*

9. $\sqrt{6} - 2$; $2\sqrt{2} - \sqrt{6}$; $\sqrt{10} - 2\sqrt{2}$; $\sqrt{10} - 2$

Lessons 6.9 and 6.10
Additional Practice

1. a. $10\sqrt{3}$ **b.** $4\sqrt{2}$

    c. $5\sqrt{2}$ **d.** $3\sqrt{6}$

    e. $2\sqrt{15}$ **f.** $8\sqrt{3}$

    g. $\sqrt{42}$ **h.** 13

2. a. $2\sqrt{41}$ in.   **b.** $\frac{5}{12}$ in.

    c. $\frac{\sqrt{5}}{4}$ in.

3. a. area: 120 cm²; perimeter: $18\sqrt{6}$ cm

    b. area: $12\sqrt{21}$ cm²;
       perimeter: $(12\sqrt{3} + 4\sqrt{7})$ cm

    c. area: 20 cm²; perimeter: $9\sqrt{10}$ cm

4. a. $4\sqrt{2}$ **b.** $9\sqrt{3}$

    c. $16\sqrt{4}$ or 32   **d.** $25\sqrt{5}$

    e. $36\sqrt{6}$

    f. For any positive number x,
       $\sqrt{x^5} = x^2\sqrt{x}$.

5. a–b. Answers may vary. Samples
       are given.

    a. Construct a right triangle with
       legs 2 units and 3 units. Drop the
       hypotenuse onto the number line.

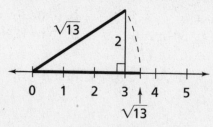

This shows that $\sqrt{13}$ is a real
number lying between 3 and 4 on
the number line.

b. Construct a right triangle with
leg 3 units, base $\sqrt{7}$ units, and
hypotenuse 4 units. Align the base
to the number line.

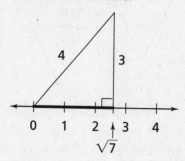

This shows that $\sqrt{7}$ is a real
number lying between 2 and 3 on
the number line.

6. a–f.

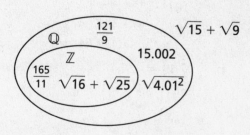

7. a. 4 and 5   **b.** 4 and 5

    c. 5 and 6   **d.** 5 and 6

    e. 5 and 6   **f.** 5 and 6

    g. 6 and 7   **h.** 7 and 8

    i. 99

Lesson 6.11 Additional Practice

1. a. Answers may vary. Samples:

x	g(x)
−3	6
−2	4
−1	2
0	0
1	2
2	4
3	6

x	h(x)
−3	−6
−2	−4
−1	−2
0	0
1	2
2	4
3	6

b. $y = \sqrt{(2x)^2}$ $y = \sqrt[3]{(2x)^3}$

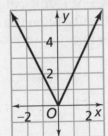 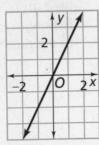

c. The functions are equal when x is zero or positive. The functions have opposite values when x is negative. The graph of $g(x)$ is identical to the graph of $y = |2x|$. The graph of $h(x)$ is identical to the graph of $y = 2x$.

2. a. $\sqrt[3]{16} \cdot \sqrt[3]{4} = 4$
$$(\sqrt[3]{16} \cdot \sqrt[3]{4})^3 = 4^3$$
$$(\sqrt[3]{16})^3 \cdot (\sqrt[3]{4})^3 = 64$$
$$16 \cdot 4 = 64$$
$$64 = 64 \ ✔$$

b. $\sqrt[4]{49} = \sqrt{7}$
$$(\sqrt[4]{49})^4 = (\sqrt{7})^4$$
$$49 = 7^2$$
$$49 = 49 \ ✔$$

c. $\sqrt[3]{6} \cdot \sqrt[6]{5} = \sqrt[6]{180}$
$$(\sqrt[3]{6} \cdot \sqrt[6]{5})^6 = (\sqrt[6]{180})^6$$
$$(\sqrt[3]{6})^6 \cdot (\sqrt[6]{5})^6 = 180$$
$$6^2 \cdot 5 = 180$$
$$36 \cdot 5 = 180$$
$$180 = 180 \ ✔$$

d. $\dfrac{\sqrt[4]{99}}{\sqrt[4]{11}} = \sqrt[4]{9}$
$$\left(\dfrac{\sqrt[4]{99}}{\sqrt[4]{11}}\right)^4 = (\sqrt[4]{9})^4$$
$$\dfrac{(\sqrt[4]{99})^4}{(\sqrt[4]{11})^4} = 9$$
$$\dfrac{99}{11} = 9$$
$$9 = 9 \ ✔$$

e. $\dfrac{\sqrt[10]{88}}{\sqrt[5]{2}} = \sqrt[10]{22}$
$$\left(\dfrac{\sqrt[10]{88}}{\sqrt[5]{2}}\right)^{10} = (\sqrt[10]{22})^{10}$$
$$\dfrac{(\sqrt[10]{88})^{10}}{(\sqrt[5]{2})^{10}} = 22$$
$$\dfrac{88}{2^2} = 22$$
$$\dfrac{88}{4} = 22$$
$$22 = 22 \ ✔$$

f. $\sqrt[5]{5} \cdot \sqrt[5]{12} \cdot \sqrt[5]{10} = \sqrt[5]{600}$
$$(\sqrt[5]{5} \cdot \sqrt[5]{12} \cdot \sqrt[5]{10})^5 = (\sqrt[5]{600})^5$$
$$(\sqrt[5]{5})^5 \cdot (\sqrt[5]{12})^5 \cdot (\sqrt[5]{10})^5 = 600$$
$$5 \cdot 12 \cdot 10 = 600$$
$$600 = 600 \ ✔$$

3. a. 1024   **b.** $64\sqrt[3]{4}$
c. 32   **d.** 16
e. $4\sqrt[6]{4^4}$ **f.** $4\sqrt[7]{4^3}$
g. $4\sqrt[8]{4^2}$ **h.** $4\sqrt[9]{4}$
i. 4
j. a, c, d, i; any root that is a factor of 10 results in an integer.

4. a. 512 ft^3; 1536 ft^3
b. If the side of the larger cube is $3 \cdot 8 = 24$ ft, then its volume would be $24^3 = 13{,}824$ ft^3. This value is not equal to the volume in part (a).
c. $8\sqrt[3]{3}$ ft or 11.54 ft

5. a. 6   **b.** 6^2 or 36
c. 6^3 or 216   **d.** 6^4 or 1296
e. 6^5 or 7776
f. If $\sqrt[n]{6} \cdot \sqrt[n]{p} = 6$, then $p = 6^{n-1}$.

Practice Workbook Answers *(continued)*

Lessons 6.13 and 6.14
Additional Practice

1.

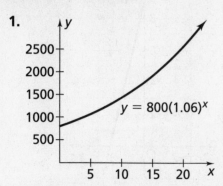

$y = 800(1.06)^x$

Answers may vary. Sample: The graph can represent the value in an investment account with an initial deposit of $800, earning 6% interest compounded annually.

2. 9 years; 14 years; 18 years

3. a. 23 years   **b.** 12 years
    c. 8 years   **d.** 6 years

4. a. $5304.50   **b.** $5307.99
    c. $5512.50   **d.** $5524.71

5. a. $624.32   **b.** $788.13
    c. $955.08   **d.** $1298.56
    e. $1655   **f.** $2024.64

6. a. $\frac{48}{64} = \frac{3}{4}, \frac{36}{48} = \frac{3}{4}, \frac{27}{36} = \frac{3}{4}$

    b. bounce 4: 20.3 ft
       bounce 5: 15.2 ft
       bounce 6: 11.4 ft

    c. $\frac{3}{4}h$

    d. $h = 64\left(\frac{3}{4}\right)^b$

7. a. 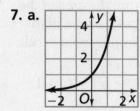   **b.**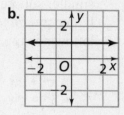

c. 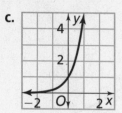   **d.**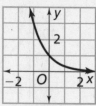

e. 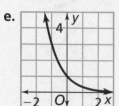   **f.**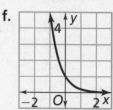

8. a. $0 < b < 1$ **b.** $b > 1$ **c.** $b = 1$

Lesson 6.15 Additional Practice

1. a. exponential; $y = 3^{-x}$
    b. neither
    c. exponential; $y = 4^{x+1}$
    d. linear; $y = 5 - 3x$

2. a. $y = 2^{-x}$
    b. $y = 2x^2$

3. a. $y = 100 - 20x$; $y = 100(0.8)^x$

    b.

x	y = 100 − 20x	Δ
0	100	20
1	80	20
2	60	20
3	40	20
4	20	20
5	0	

x	y = 100(0.8)^x	÷
0	100	0.8
1	80	0.8
2	64	0.8
3	51.2	0.8
4	40.96	0.8
5	32.77	

c.

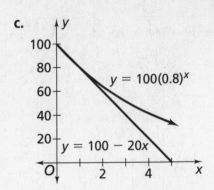

$y = 100(0.8)^x$

$y = 100 - 20x$

4. a. 6   **b.** 1
   c. 11   **d.** −3
   e. 17   **f.** −23

5. a. 9   **b.** 21
   c. 0   **d.** −15
   e. 5   **f.** 17
   g. 13   **h.** 25
   i. 8   **j.** 20
   k. 7   **l.** 19

6. a.

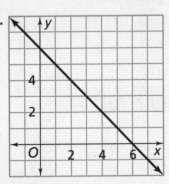

b.

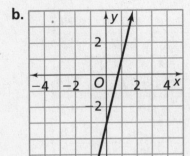

c.

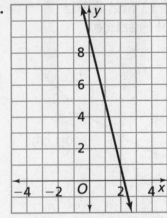

d.

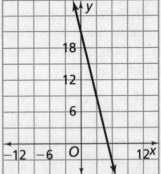

Chapter 7

Lessons 7.2 and 7.3
Additional Practice

1. a. −18, 17   **b.** −22, 21
   c. −13, 14

2. a. −10   **b.** −210
   c. −810   **d.** $p(x) = -8x^2 - 10$

3. $(x^2 + 2x - y^2 - 2y)$ in.^{2}; square the
side lengths to find the area of each
square. Subtract the area of the
smaller square from the area of the
larger square to get the area of the
leftover shape. Simplify your result.

$$(x + 1)^2 - (y + 1)^2$$
$$= x^2 + 2x + 1 - (y^2 + 2y + 1)$$
$$= x^2 + 2x - y^2 - 2y$$

Practice Workbook Answers *(continued)*

4. Expand $q(x)$ to show that it is the same as $p(x)$.

$$q(x) = (x^2 + x - 1)(x^2 - x - 1)$$
$$= x^4 - x^3 - x^2 + x^3 - x^2 -$$
$$x - x^2 + x + 1$$
$$= x^4 - 3x^2 + 1$$

5. a. $-3, 8$ **b.** $-12, 11$
   c. $0, 6$ **d.** $2, 3, 4$

6. $-1, 0, 1$

7. a. $-27, -19$ **b.** $-47, -13$
   c. $-1, \frac{4}{3}$ **d.** $0, -\frac{5}{12}$

8. a. $x^2 + (5 + 8)x + (5 \cdot 8)$
   b. $p = 4, q = 7$ or $p = 7, q = 4$

9. a. $(x - 4)(x + 7) = 0$
     or $x^2 + 3x - 28 = 0$
   b. $(x + 4)(x - 7) = 0$
     or $x^2 - 3x - 28 = 0$
   c. $(x + 4)(x + 7) = 0$
     or $x^2 + 11x + 28 = 0$
   d. $x(x + 4)(x + 7) = 0$
     or $x^3 + 11x^2 + 28x = 0$

Lesson 7.4 Additional Practice

1. a. $2x^2$ **b.** $10x$
   c. 9 **d.** p
   e. mn **f.** a^2

2. a. $2x^2(5x^2 - 9)$ **b.** $10x(x^3 + 4)$
   c. $9(2p^3 - 3q^2)$ **d.** $p(q + r)$
   e. $mn(m - n)$
   f. $a^2(ab^3 - b^2 - c^2)$

3. a. $x = 0$ or $x = -\frac{4}{5}$ **b.** $x = 0$ or $p = 5$
   c. $x = 0$ or $x = \frac{5}{2}$ **d.** $x = 0$ or $x = 64$
   e. $x = 0$ or $x = \pm 2$ **f.** $x = 0$ and $y = 0$

4. a. $(4x - 1)(5x + 6)$
   b. $(2x - 3)(3x + 5)$

5. a. $y(4p - 7q)$ **b.** $x^2(4p - 7q)$
   c. $(x - 3)(4p + 7q)$ **d.** $4x^2(p - 2q)$
   e. $(x - 3)(4p + 7q)$ **f.** $(r + s)(p + 1)$

6. The coordinate points at $x = a$ and $x = b$ are (a, a^2) and (b, b^2). So the vertical distance d is equal to $b^2 - a^2$, or $(b - a)(b + a)$.

7. a. $x^6 - 2x^5 + 1$
   b. $x^7 - 2x^6 + 1$
   c. $x^8 - 2x^7 + 1$
   d. $x^9 - x^8 - x^7 - x^6 - x^5 - x^4 - x^3 - x^2 - x - 1$

Lessons 7.6 and 7.7 Additional Practice

1. a–d. Answers may vary. Samples are given.
   a. $2x^2 + 6x - 7$ and $-x^2 - x + 4$
   b. $x^2 + 3x - 1$ and $2x - 2$
   c. $x^2 + 2x - 5$ and $-x^2 - 2x - 5$
   d. $x + 4$ and $x - 4$

2. a. $2x^2 - 8x + 2$
   b. $x^2 + 3x - 11$
   c. Answers may vary. Sample: $2x + 1$

3. 3

4. a. $-2x + 1$
   b. $-3x^2 + 3x - 1$
   c. $-4x^3 + 6x^2 - 4x + 1$
   d. $x^2 - 2xy$
   e. $x^3 - 3x^2y + 3xy^2 - 2y^3$
   f. $x^4 - 4x^3y + 6x^2y^2 - 4xy^3$
   g. x^2
   h. $x^3 - x$
   i. $x^3 - 4x$

5. $x^4 + 4x^3 + (b - 1)x^2 + (2b - 10)x - 5b; b = 5$

Practice Workbook Answers (continued)

6. a. $x^{10} - 4 = (x^5 + 2)(x^5 - 2)$
$= x^{10} - 2x^5 + 2x^5 - 4$
$= x^{10} - 4$

b. $x^3 + 1 = (x + 1)(x^2 - x + 1)$
$= x^3 - x^2 + x + x^2 - x + 1$
$= x^3 + 1$

c. $8ab = (a + 2b)^2 - (a - 2b)^2$
$= (a^2 + 4ab + 4b^2) -$
$(a^2 - 4ab + 4b^2)$
$= 8ab$

d. $3n + 1 = (n + 1)^3 - n^2(n + 3)$
$= (n + 1)(n^2 + 2n + 1) -$
$n^3 - 3n^2$
$= n^3 + 2n^2 + n + n^2 +$
$2n + 1 - n^3 - 3n^2$
$= 3n + 1$

e. Factor both sides of the equation to get $x(x + 2)(x - 2)$.

f. Factor both sides of the equation to get $x(x + a)(x - a)$.

7. a–b. Answers may vary. Samples are given:

a. Factor both sides of the equation to get $(2a + b)(2a - b)$.

b. The terms on the left side of the equation have the common factor $(2a - b)$. So the left side can be factored as $(2a + 1 + b - 1)(2a - b)$. Simplifying gives $(2a + b)(2a - b)$. This is the same as the right side of the equation.

8. a. $x^5 + x^4 - x^3 - x^2 - x + 1$
b. $x^7 + x^6 + x^5 - x^4 - x^3 - x^2 - x + 1$

Lesson 7.8 Additional Practice

1. a. -4 **b.** 10   **c.** 0

2. 5

3. 15

4. 16

5. a. 1   **b.** 1   **c.** 1   **d.** 1

6. a. -1 **b.** 2   **c.** 3

d. -1 **e.** 3   **f.** 3

7. a. $x^3 + 1$
b. $x^5 + 1$
c. $x^7 + 1$

8. a. $x^5 + x^4 + x^3 + x^2 + x + 1$
b. $x^{17} + x^{16} + x^{15} + x^{14} + x^{13} + x^{12} + x^{11} + x^{10} + x^9 + x^8 + x^7 + x^6 + x^5 + x^4 + x^3 + x^2 + x + 1$
c. $x^{20} + x^{19} + x^{18} + x^{17} + x^{16} + x^{15} + x^{14} + x^{13} + x^{12} + x^{11} + x^{10} + x^9 + x^8 + x^7 + x^6 + x^5 + x^4 + x^3 + x^2 + x + 1$

Lessons 7.10 and 7.11 Additional Practice

1. a. 0; multiply the terms together to get $(15 + p)(15 - p) = 225 - p^2$. The greatest possible product is 225, when p is zero.
b. $p = 15, q = 15$

2. a. $y = -4$ or $y = 4$
b. $y = -1$ or $y = 11$
c. $y = \frac{1}{3}$ or $y = 1$
d. $y = \frac{1}{a} + \frac{1}{b}$ or $y = \frac{1}{a} - \frac{1}{b}$

3. a. Yes; $z^{10} - 100 = (z^5)^2 - (10)^2$, so it can be factored as $(z^5 + 10)(z^5 - 10)$.
b. 10
c. 5; 5; 10

4. a. $x = -5$ or $x = 5$
b. $x = -7$ or $x = 7$
c. $x = -\sqrt{5}$ or $x = \sqrt{5}$
d. no real numbers
e. no real numbers
f. no real numbers
g. $x = -3$ or $x = 3$
h. $x = -2\sqrt{2}$ or $x = 2\sqrt{2}$
i. no real numbers

5. a. 23   **b.** 23   **c.** 19

Practice Workbook Answers *(continued)*

d. Each expression is in the form $a^2 - b^2$, so it can be factored as $(a + b)(a - b)$. The term $(a + b)$, if it is prime, is the largest prime factor of the original number.

6. a. $x = 3$ or $x = 8$ **b.** $x = 7$
  c. $x = -5$ **d.** $x = 0$ or $x = 11$
  e. $x = -1$ or $x = -6$
  f. $x = 2$ or $x = 8$

7. a. no **b.** yes; $(x - 12)^2$
  c. yes; $(x + 16)^2$ **d.** yes; $(x - 21)^2$
  e. no **f.** no

8. a. $(x + 6)(x + 6)$
  b. $(x + 20)(x - 20)$
  c. $(x + 1)(x + 8)$
  d. $(x + 8)(x + 4)$
  e. Not factorable; you cannot take the square root of a negative number.
  f. Not factorable; no integers multiply to 10 and have a sum of 9.
  g. $(x + 1)(x + 11)$
  h. $(x + 1)(x + 399)$
  i. $(x + 3)(x + 6)$

9. a. $x = -5$ or $x = -7$
  b. $x = -2$ or $x = -10$
  c. No solution; no integers multiply to -35 and have a sum of 12.
  d. No solution; no integers multiply to -20 and have a sum of 12.

Lesson 7.12 Additional Practice

1. a. 3 **b.** 4
  c. 3.5 **d.** 5.5

2. a. 48 **b.** 25

3. a. $x = 1$ or $x = 9$
  b. $x = -1$ or $x = \frac{2}{3}$
  c. $x = -2 - \sqrt{11}$ or $x = -2 + \sqrt{11}$
  d. $x = 6 - \sqrt{37}$ or $x = 6 + \sqrt{37}$
  e. $x = -5$ or $x = 1$
  f. $x = -6$ or $x = 6$

4.
$$x^2 - 12x - 5 = 8$$
$$x^2 - 12x - 13 = 0$$
$$(x^2 - 12x + 36) - 49 = 0$$
$$(x - 6)^2 - 7^2 = 0$$
$$((x - 6) + 7)((x - 6) - 7) = 0$$
$$(x + 1)(x - 13) = 0$$
$$x = -1 \text{ or } x = 13$$

5. a. $x = 5 + 3\sqrt{5}$ or $x = 5 - 3\sqrt{5}$
  b. $x = -6 - 4\sqrt{11}$ or $x = -6 + 4\sqrt{11}$
  c. $x = -27$ or $x = 7$
  d. $x = 3 - \sqrt{186}$ or $x = 3 + \sqrt{186}$

6. a.

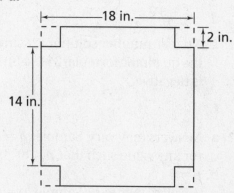

b. 2 in. by 2 in.; let the length of the side of a cut square be x inches. The bottom area is 196 in.^{2}, giving the equation $(18 - 2x)(18 - 2x) = 196$. Expanding and combining like terms gives $4x^2 - 72x + 128 = 0$. Solve for x by dividing by 4 and factoring.
$$x^2 - 18x + 32 = 0$$
$$(x - 2)(x - 16) = 0$$
$$x = 2 \text{ or } x = 16$$

From the diagram in part (a), the length of the side of a cut square cannot be 16 in. So, the side length of a cut square is 2 in.

c. 324 in.^{2}; 4 in.^{2}

7. a. $+36$ **b.** $+36$ **c.** $+\frac{81}{4}$

d. $+\frac{81}{4}$ **e.** $+144$ **f.** $+\frac{1}{4}$

g. $+\frac{b^2}{4}$ **h.** $+\frac{b^2}{4}$ **i.** $+\frac{b^2}{16}$

Chapter 8

Lesson 8.2 Additional Practice

1. a. $-\frac{1}{2}, 3$ **b.** $-1, -\frac{3}{2}$

c. 1.5

d. $\frac{-3 + 3\sqrt{2}}{2}, \frac{-3 - 3\sqrt{2}}{2}$

e. No real-number solutions; using the quadratic formula, $2^2 - 4(3)(10)$ is negative.

f. $1, -\frac{3}{2}$

2. a. Answers may vary. Sample: $p = 7$ (or any value such that $p < 8$)

b. $p = 8$

c. Answers may vary. Sample: $p = 9$ (or any value such that $p > 8$)

3. a. $\frac{3 - \sqrt{149}}{10} < x < \frac{3 + \sqrt{149}}{10}$

b. $x < \frac{3 - \sqrt{149}}{10}$ or $x > \frac{3 + \sqrt{149}}{10}$

c. $x = \frac{3 - \sqrt{149}}{10}$ or $x = \frac{3 + \sqrt{149}}{10}$

4. a. $x = 0$

b. $x = \frac{45 + \sqrt{1961}}{4}$ or $x = \frac{45 - \sqrt{1961}}{4}$

5 a. $x^2 - 5x - 14 = 0$

b. Answers may vary. Sample:
$2x^2 - 10x - 28 = 0$,
$3x^2 - 15x - 42 = 0$

c. $x^2 + 5x - 14 = 0$

d. Answers may vary. Sample:
$2x^2 + 10x - 28 = 0$,
$3x^2 + 15x - 42 = 0$

6. a. $\frac{3 + \sqrt{-11}}{2}, \frac{3 - \sqrt{-11}}{2}$

b. $3 + \sqrt{-6}, 3 - \sqrt{-6}$

c. $\frac{1 + \sqrt{-7}}{2}, \frac{1 - \sqrt{-7}}{2}$

7. a. $\frac{7 \pm \sqrt{41}}{2}$; sum is 7, product is 2.

b. $\frac{10 \pm \sqrt{92}}{2}$; sum is 10, product is 2.

c. $\frac{-10 \pm \sqrt{68}}{2}$; sum is -10, product is 8.

d. $\frac{1}{2}, 2$; sum is 2.5, product is 1.

e. $\frac{-p \pm \sqrt{p^2 - 4t}}{2}$; sum is $-p$, product is t.

f. $\frac{-10 \pm \sqrt{20}}{2}$; sum is -10, product is 20.

g. For the equation $ax^2 + bx + c = 0$, the sum is the value $-\frac{b}{a}$ and the product is the value $\frac{c}{a}$.

Lessons 8.3 and 8.4 Additional Practice

1. a. $x^2 - 16x + 48 = 0$
b. $x^2 + 16x + 48 = 0$
c. $x^2 - 49x + 328 = 0$
d. $x^2 - 6x + 4 = 0$
e. $x^2 + 8x + 9 = 0$
f. $x^2 - 18x + 63 = 0$

2. a. $-\frac{2}{3}$ **b.** $-\frac{8}{3}$ **c.** $-\frac{1}{3}$

3. a. $x = \frac{5}{7}$ or $x = \frac{9}{8}$

b. $(7x - 5)(8x - 9)$

c. $x = \frac{4}{13}$ or $x = \frac{23}{12}$

d. $(13x - 4)(12x - 23)$

e. For quadratics with rational roots, use the quadratic formula to find the two roots, $\frac{m}{p}$ and $\frac{n}{q}$. The factored quadratic equation over $\mathbb{Z}$ is $(px - m)(qx - n)$.

4. a. $(4x + 1)(4x - 9)$
  b. $(5x - 7)(5x - 1)$
  c. $(25x - 14)(x + 1)$
  d. $(25x - 7)(x + 2)$
  e. $(16x - 3)(x + 1)$
  f. $(16x^2 - 3)(x^2 + 1)$

5. a. $(4x + y)(4x - 9y)$
  b. $(5x - 7y)(5x - y)$
  c. $(25x - 14y)(x + y)$
  d. $(25x - 7y)(x + 2y)$

6. a. $-(10x + 1)(2x + 7)$
  b. $-(10x + 1)(2x - 7)$
  c. $(7 - 10x)(7 + 10x)$
  d. $x(10x + 1)(2x - 7)$

7. a. $(8x - 1)(x + 3)$
  b. $(4x - 1)(2x + 3)$
  c. $(4x - 3)(2x + 1)$
  d. $(4x + 1)(2x + 3)$
  e. $(8x^2 - 1)(x^2 + 3)$
  f. $(8x^2 - 32x + 31)(x^2 - 4x + 7)$
  g. $(2x^2 + x + 2)(2x^2 - x + 4)$

8. $x = -3$ or $x = \frac{2}{3}$

Lesson 8.6 Additional Practice

1. a. $y = -7$ **b.** $y = -9$
  c. $y = -56.25$

2. Answers may vary. Sample:
  $y = x^2 - 15$

3. 16 and 16

4. 87.5 and 87.5

5. 500.5 and 500.5

6. -80

7. a. 52 ft-by-52 ft
  b. 52 ft-by-104 ft

8. -1

9. -4

10. $f(-4 + 1) = f(-3) = 0$;
  $f(-4 - 1) = f(-5) = 0$

11. $f(-4 + 2) = f(-2) = 3$;
  $f(-4 - 2) = f(-6) = 3$

12. If $f(m)$ is the minimum value of a quadratic function and a is any real number, then $f(m + a) = f(m - a)$.

Lessons 8.7 and 8.8 Additional Practice

1. a. $(-5, 4)$; $x = -5$

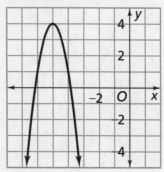

b. $(3, -5)$; $x = 3$

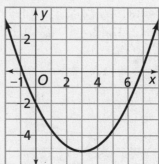

c. $(-3, -7)$; $x = -3$

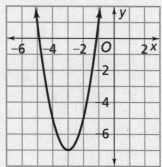

d. $(6, 5)$; $x = 6$

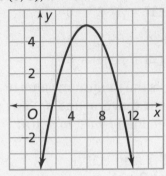

e. $(-2, 4)$; $x = -2$

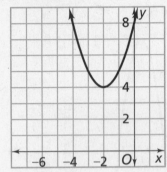

2. a. $(8, 0)$ **b.** $y = -x^2 + 8x$

3. a. Answers may vary. Sample:
$(0, 0), (2, 1), (2, -1), (8, 2), (8, -2),$
$(18, 3), (18, -3)$

b.

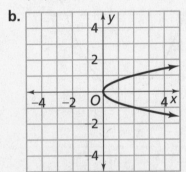

4. a. $x(36 - x)$

b. The graph of $y = -x^2 + 36x$ has roots 0 and 36. So the axis of symmetry is $x = \frac{0 + 36}{2} = 18$, and the maximum value of the graph occurs at $x = 18$.

c. $y = -(x - 18)^2 + 324$

5. a. $(5, 10)$

    b. $y = 3(x - 5)^2 + 10$

    c. 85

6. $\left(3, \frac{44}{3}\right)$

7. $x = -10$ or $x = -6$

8. Answers may vary. Sample:
$y = 2x^2 + 16x + 5,$
$y = -2x^2 - 16x + 1,$
$y = 3x^2 + 24x$

9. a. $(5, -25)$ **b.** $c = 25$

    c. $(5, 22)$ **d.** $(5, -25 + c)$

10. a. $c = 36$ **b.** $c = 16$

    c. $c = 64$ **d.** $(11, 0)$

    e. $(-11, -128)$

Lessons 8.10 and 8.11
Additional Practice

1. a. 2   **b.** 1   **c.** 0

    d. 1   **e.** 0   **f.** 1

    g. 2   **h.** 1   **i.** 1

2. a. a horizontal line through $(0, 10)$

    b. $x = -3$ or $x = 5$

    c. $-3 < x < 5$

    d. $x < -3$ or $x > 5$

3. a.

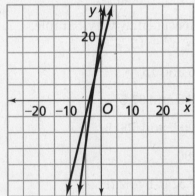

b.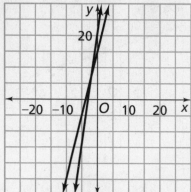

c.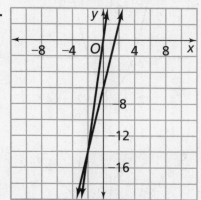

d.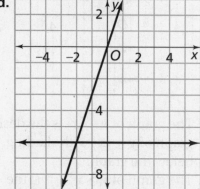

e.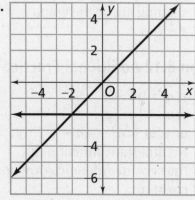

4. a.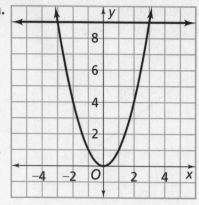

b.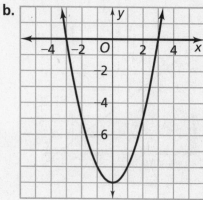

5. a.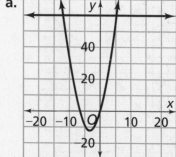

b.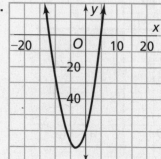

189

6. a. 2 solutions

b. $x = -6.9$ or $x = 0.9$

7. a.

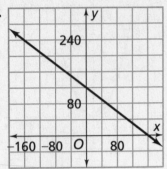

b.

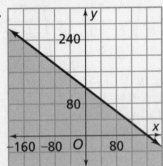

8. a.

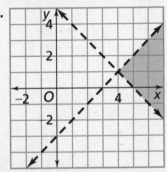

b.

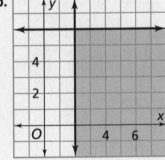

c.

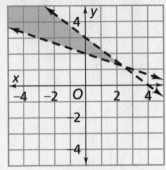

d.

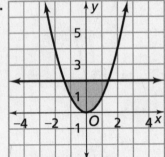

e.

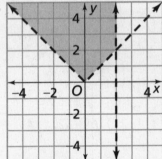

9. a. The graph of $y < |x|$ is the dashed graph of $y = |x|$ with shading below the graph.

b. The graph of $y > x^3 + 7$ is the dashed graph of $y = x^3 + 7$ with shading above the graph.

c. $y \geq f(x)$

Lesson 8.12 Additional Practice

1. a. $y(n) = n^2 + n - 3$

b. $y(n) = (n - 2)^2$
or $y(n) = n^2 - 4n + 4$

c. No quadratic function fits; the second differences are not constant.

Practice Workbook Answers *(continued)*

2. a. No; the second differences are not constant.

b. Yes; the second differences are constant.

3. a. $b(n) = 5x^2 - 3x + 6$

b. $c(n) = -2n^2 + 11n - 10$

4.

Input	Output	Δ	Δ^2	Δ^3
0	3	16	4	7
1	19	20	11	9
2	39	31	20	8
3	70	51	28	
4	121	79		
5	200			

Since none of the differences are constant, the table does not match a linear, quadratic, or cubic function.

5. a.

x	f(x)
0	14
1	6
2	0
3	−4
4	−6
5	−6

b.

x	g(x)
0	8
1	3
2	0
3	−1
4	0
5	3

c.

x	h(x)
0	0
1	8
2	18
3	30
4	44
5	60

d.

x	j(x)
0	−6
1	0
2	10
3	24
4	42
5	64

e. Answers may vary. Sample:

x	k(x)
0	2
1	0
2	0
3	2
4	6
5	12